WORSHIP
and the Ear of God

DAVE HARDY

All Scripture quotations are taken from the King James Version.

Published by
The Global Baptist Times
PO Box 1985
Stillwater, OK 74076
www.baptisttimes.org

Worship and the Ear of God
Stillwater, Oklahoma
ISBN: 978-1-939823-18-2

Edited by Kandra Stukenborg and Harry Hix and Carol Hix
Cover Illustration by Brenda Snodderly
Layout by Amanda Howerton

Printed in the United States of America

Dedication

This book is dedicated first to my son, Wayne Hardy, who from a young age has had a heart for God and God's people. His heart is visible in his dedication not only to the Lord's work but also to the Person of God in biblical worship. Second, the book is dedicated to the faithful members of Bible Baptist Church in Stillwater, Oklahoma, who eagerly and joyfully kneel in corporate worship every Sunday morning during our worship time.

Acknowledgements

Thank you to my wife who has been a constant source of encouragement in all our ministry endeavors. To Hannah Schmutzler who particularly pushed me to put these thoughts on paper. To Kandra Stukenborg for typing the manuscript as well as research and overall coordination. To Harry and Carol Hix for hours of labor in editing and providing valuable suggestions. To Amanda Howerton for the typesetting and coordination with Robert Greenlaw and David Owen of Kimray, Inc. for printing. Also, to others too numerous to mention, but who made their own unique contributions.

Table of Contents

A Parable of Worship

I watched in wonder as my son held his first grandchild, looking into his eyes. Lincoln, just two weeks old, stared into my son's eyes intently. There they were, my 53-year-old son and my newborn great-grandson, with their eyes locked on each other. Neither was interested in anything else going on around them. No words in my vocabulary can adequately describe that scene. There was love, admiration, fascination, astonishment, curiosity, and maybe some awe. Part of what was taking place was captured in a picture, but more was taking place that is beyond photography. I could only revel in the occasion.

If you have children, grandchildren, or great-grandchildren, you may have similar images in your own mind. God gave these precious gifts to us for our enjoyment and maybe for our learning. In the aforementioned moment, my son's eyes exuded an overwhelming, unconditional love. It was a love that little Lincoln could in no way comprehend. This full-grown man was so much larger, stronger, and wiser than Lincoln. Nevertheless, there was something being transferred back and forth between the two that neither could fully understand. There was something—no matter how miniscule it may have been—in Lincoln's mind, and his gaze into my son's face was captivating. That interaction reminds me of worship between God and His children. True worship is a time when the All-knowing and the begotten come together.

Even now, after much time has passed, God uses that scene I witnessed to teach me. It causes me to think about my time with my Heavenly Father, when I bow before Him with my face in my hands and the world closed out.

Sometimes there are words, and sometimes there are just thoughts. It is an intimate time to just be still and know that He is God, that He loves me, and that I have great favor in His eyes. Like Lincoln, I behold the One who holds me in His hands, but my comprehension of Him is virtually nil in comparison to all that He is. However, unlike my son, my Heavenly Father looks at me with total understanding of my innermost being and thoughts of Him.

In the coming years, my son and his grandson will grow in their relationship with each other. They will someday talk with each other and do things together. Before Lincoln was born, his grandfather already knew about him and awaited his arrival. Now, he will wait longer and earnestly look forward to their years together. As Lincoln grows, my son will yearn for a loving relationship with him and will *always* be interested in what is happening in his life. Mark it down—my son will have an attentive ear for that little boy. It is a beautiful picture that only God can draw, revealing His ear for His own.

Oh, what a wonderful start here, but it isn't the end of the story, is it? What lies ahead for my son and Lincoln? If their relationship grows, as it should, it will only get better. My son might think he could never love him more than he does now, but he surely will. How do I know this? It is because of my own grandchildren and my love for them! My son will have no need for anything material that Lincoln could offer, but he will greatly desire his affection.

Reaching a time that I would not love my son, my grandchildren, my great-grandchildren, or anyone in our family is beyond my thinking process. However, my love for them needs to be reciprocal for it to work as God planned. My three grandchildren are fine young adults. All are saved and love the Lord. They love and honor their parents and their grandparents. They are respected by their peers and older adults, which only accents my joy. My son and I had special times together over the years—just the two of us. The only way those times could have been better is if there had been more of them. The same is true of our grandchildren. My wife and I often spent time with all three at once, but we worked at having them one at a time, as well. It was a special one-on-one time for us.

I don't know that the interaction I saw between my son and his first grandson can be adequately described, but it was priceless and remains embedded in my mind. If that is true, with my son's limited ability to love, what is it like with God's love? That beautiful picture could have never been if Lincoln had just squirmed and screamed the whole time. With everything that is within me, including my limited ability, I want that trusting, peaceful, communing relationship with my Heavenly Father. And, as needy as I am, I want to have that special one-on-one time in worship of Him and to know that I have His ear. Have you ever given serious thought to how you worship God and how much it means to Him? Have you ever considered how much it may endear Him to you and you to Him?

God is self-existent and self-sufficient. He owns the cattle on a thousand hills. He can literally speak into existence anything He chooses. He needs nothing man owns. However, Scripture says there is something we have to offer that is special to Him—something that He treasures. I think it is something similar to what happened between my son and Lincoln. The focus of that little two-week-old boy, gazing into his Papa's face, was a unique gift from him that no one else could give. That is exactly the nature of worship. Lincoln wasn't asking for anything or even giving thanks for previous blessings. He was just wholly taken up with the one holding him. In return, the one holding him would have given Lincoln anything—including his life.

Chapter One
The Journey to Worship Begins

I grew up in a Christian home and have been privileged to be a Christian since 1958. When I was fourteen, I came to an understanding of salvation in Christ. I trusted Him and surrendered my life to do whatever He would bid me. I clearly remember the night I was saved. I remember the message that was preached from John 5:24 and the special music that was sung, "Now I Belong to Jesus." I think my heart was pure—but not sinless—in those early years, as I endeavored to find my way through life in a way pleasing to Him. I was faithful to church and abstained from quite a number of activities that I believed were not in keeping with my faith. Of course, I fell short in numerous ways, many of which I did not recognize until later.

God was good in directing my path as a teenager at home, then in marriage, and later while serving on a submarine in the U.S. Navy. He guided me to good churches and fellow believers to help me grow spiritually. It was in one of those churches that God introduced me to a special young lady, custom-made to be my life partner, to whom I've been married for fifty-five years. My debt to those people, especially the pastors, is greater than I can ever repay. I can only hope to return the help to someone else along the way.

Having mentioned the benefits that have come my way from churches and pastors, I have to say that there was at least one area that I missed, and it was an important one. It was worship. I suppose you could say I was involved in some form of personal worship, since I always knelt by my bed at night to pray. However, it would have benefitted me greatly if my church had practiced corporate worship and had explained the concept of worship to me.

Most of the churches I attended over the years displayed a sign out front with a schedule of the services. These were also listed in the bulletin. Normally, the schedule listed the following services:

Sunday School at 10:00 a.m.

Worship Service at 11:00 a.m.

Sunday Evening Service at 6:00 p.m.

Wednesday Night Prayer and Bible Study at 7:00 p.m.

I attended and enjoyed them all for years and never gave much thought to their claims.

In 1989, while pastoring Eastland Baptist Church in Tulsa, Oklahoma, and taking some Doctor of Ministry courses at Dallas Theological Seminary, the subject of worship aroused my interest. Then it did more. First, it convicted me heavily and then almost consumed me. It was as if I realized I had been missing something for which I was created. Douglas Horton said, "Man worships because God lays His hand to the dust of our experience, and man miraculously becomes a living soul—and knows it and wants to worship."[1] It wasn't that I had not endeavored to honor the Lord, but I just knew so little about worship. I had to face the fact that I did not have a definition of worship that was acceptable—even to me. I could not bear my failure because of the indescribable God Who had done all and given all for me. I literally wept as I thought about my withholding the worship He desired and deserved.

Looking back on the schedule of services—the Sunday morning worship service in particular—I had to ask myself, "What makes it a worship service?" All I could come up with was that the sign said that was what happened during that timeframe, and that it was maybe a little more formal than the other services preceding and following it. I kept wondering what was different about that service that set it apart from the Sunday evening one or the Wednesday evening one. What qualified it to be a worship service? I could see nothing truly defining. It would have been far more accurate to call it a preaching service, which some churches do.

How is it that so many churches advertise something they may not have or may not do? I do not believe it was, or is, an intentional misrepresentation but rather a lack of understanding. Yet it seems to me that God has somehow preserved the idea of worship in our hearts, or, if not in our hearts, then somewhere else in our being. Worship is important to every sovereign, and how much more so to our Sovereign—God Himself.

You may have already noted the brevity of this work. You may ask, "If this is a big deal, why is it so brief?" First, I question my ability to make the minutest contribution to this hallowed subject, much less a thorough treatment. Second, there are a number of good works, more exhaustive, from which to draw. Third, I borrow the idiom: "You can't see the forest for the trees." The brevity of this book may be likened to an owner's manual for a car, as compared to a service manual for mechanics. If new car owners had to read and comprehend the large service manual, they might rethink buying a car. They may rather keep their old mode of transportation—or even walk—than face the complexity of this new machine. It could be similar with worship. It must be simple, kept on the lower shelf, lest the simplest of God's people be discouraged from this wonderful opportunity.

Chapter Two

Worship and the Ear of God

Right up front, I have to concede that I am convinced that biblical worship strengthens and deepens our relationship with the Father. This is not to discount the benefits of prayer, praise, or other acts of love, which are many. Like any good father, our Heavenly Father wants to hear from His children. I am always glad to hear from my son. He may ask me if I can help him with a project or if he can borrow a tool. He may call just to ask my thoughts on a particular situation. There have been many of those occasions, and I was always happy to be involved. In addition to that, however, I highly treasure the *many* notes he has written. Some were on Father's Day, often in the flyleaf of a book. At other times, it was a letter, for no particular occasion. The notes were about what I had meant to him as a dad. I am aware that I fell short many times, but he always had something to say about a benefit that was his because of me. I still have those notes, many written years ago.

My point is this: all of God's sons and daughters have needs, and He is very accommodating. He is the one and only Father who has it all. But shouldn't there be a special time when we honor Him for Who He is? We cannot buy Him a book or send Him a letter, but is there something He would treasure that we can give? There is. We can pray to Him, and we can praise Him, but we will never be closer than when we worship Him. When we kneel before Him, it is a one-on-one time with everything and everyone else closed out. We can gain God's attention in effectual prayer and praise, but if you want that special closeness, choose worship. You may find that you have His ear more than ever before.

Abraham had that special relationship with God. He is the first person to whom the word *worship* is ascribed. What we learn from him—as a person, from his family, and from his dealings with God—is of immeasurable value. I never tire of reading about his pilgrimage and the myriad lessons to be learned from him. Abraham certainly had the ear of God, and part of that may be because God had Abraham's ear. When God spoke to him in Genesis 12 about leaving all that he had known, Abraham was listening.

God did not always respond to Abraham within a moment's notice. However, He always did respond, and His response was never too late to serve the better purpose. Isaac may have been a long time in coming, but he came, nonetheless. Before God destroyed Sodom and Gomorrah, He spoke to Abraham about it, and Abraham interceded for the people living there. Abraham asked God if He would spare the city if fifty righteous people could be found. God listened and honored that request. Unfortunately (you know the rest of the story), fifty righteous people could not be found! A lengthy exchange ensued between Abraham and God as the number was reduced, little by little, all the way down to ten. Abraham had God's ear at every step, and God responded positively to every request.

If you are familiar with the biblical account of Abraham and his conversations with God, you know there was something special in their relationship. In spite of this, the biblical account makes it plain that Abraham had a number of failures in his life as well. I simply mention this to remind us that God did not require perfection of him. But a cursory reading of Genesis 12 and other sections of Scripture reveals that Abraham was committed to building altars to meet with God (Gen. 12:7, 8; 13:4; 22:9). Altars are for sacrifice and worship. It was Abraham's relationship with God that gained him a hearing—not his much speaking, like that of the heathen as recorded in Matthew 6:7. That passage is reminiscent of I Kings 18:21–40 with its account of the standoff between Elijah and the prophets of Baal. They cried unto Baal all morning with no response. At noon Elijah mocked them and their God. They continued their antics until the time of the evening sacrifice, yet it gained them nothing. Then Elijah repaired the altar of the Lord—a place for sacrifice and worship. Following that, he spoke for approximately thirty seconds, and the fire fell and consumed the sacrifice.

One of the most amazing statements about Abraham is found in James 2:23. The Bible says, "And the scripture was fulfilled which saith, Abraham believed God, and it was imputed unto him for righteousness: and he was called the Friend of God."

I am thankful that I have many friends. Some are as close as family to me. However, I cannot bring myself to claim to be known as the friend of God. I would like this to be said of me, but only He can give that distinction. On the other hand, He has certainly been a Friend to me.

One major characteristic of friendship is communication. Each has the other's ear. Abraham's faith is well noted and certainly holds a place in his relationship with God and having God's ear. However, do not miss the fact that Abraham's faith required an object. That object was God. God was his substance of things hoped for when there was no visible evidence. Let's say it this way: **Who God was** and **What God was** were enough for Abraham. We all face times in life when God is the only One who can help us. What is the ear of God worth then?

Another account of worship and someone having access to the ear of God is found in Matthew 15:21–28. When Jesus entered the coasts of Tyre and Sidon, a woman approached Him concerning her daughter who was "… grievously vexed with a devil." In verses 23 and 24, she was unable to get a hearing from Jesus or His disciples. In verse 25, she "worshipped him, saying, Lord, help me." Still her request was unanswered, but she had gained a hearing. Jesus then explained to her that He was sent primarily to the Jews and that it wasn't right for Him to deviate from that work. The example He used was that of a man taking food from his kids and feeding the dogs. It was a picture of the household pet hanging around for scraps. She agreed but reminded Him that the dogs got the leftover crumbs that fell from the table. Here, then, was a great revelation of her evaluation of the Lord. The act of worship had already illustrated His worth to her, but another dimension was added when she basically said, "You are so powerful that I do not need much. Just a crumb from You would be more than enough to meet my daughter's need."

When a leper threw himself at Jesus' feet and worshipped Him, He responded by healing the man immediately (Matt. 8:2, 3). Jairus, a synagogue official, worshipped the Lord, and He raised his daughter from the dead (Matt. 9:18–25). Jesus readily received worship and responded to it.

As in the story of Abraham, what the Lord could and would do was premised on who and what He was. He commended the aforementioned woman for her great faith, but that great faith could only be possible when based on a great God. Keep in mind that people respond to, and are drawn to, things or people whom they like and whom they desire. God seeks people to worship Him (John 4:23).

Chapter Three

A Definition of Worship

As mentioned previously, every attempt will be made to keep this great subject on the bottom shelf, so that it is easily accessible to those who are not familiar with the languages. I am a simple person, and I offer a simple definition though still based on the word in the original languages.

Worship is the voluntary humbling of one person, physically and spiritually, in order to exalt another.

Do I think this is a full definition or that there is no other way to worship or that nothing else could be considered worship? **Absolutely not!** However, unlike words that are used only once in the Old or New Testament, *worship* is an oft-used word, and it speaks very well for itself. Bowing, kneeling, and humbling make up the primary meaning. I have intentionally chosen to emphasize this meaning of the word because it should be emphasized and because this particular meaning seems to get lost in broader definitions of worship. Additions to the definition of the word may be in order, but any subtractions from the idea of humbling ourselves should be viewed with suspicion. Since the word does speak for itself, let's listen in for a moment.

"The vocabulary for worship in the Bible is very extensive, but the essential concept in the Bible is service and originally signified the labor of slaves or hired servants. And in order to offer this 'worship' to God, His servants must prostrate and thus manifest reverential fear and adoring awe and wonder."[1]

The first mention of *shachah*, the Hebrew word for worship, is found in Genesis 18:2 where Abraham "bowed himself toward the ground" before the three men who came as messengers announcing that Sarah would have a son. Note that the first translation of this word is not *worship*, but *bow*.

The second time, in Genesis 22:5, it is translated *worship*, even though it is the same word. This act of bowing down in homage was usually done before a superior or a ruler. David bowed before Saul (I Sam. 24:8); Ruth bowed down to the ground before Boaz (Ruth 2:10); and Joseph saw his brothers bowing down before his sheaf in a dream (Gen. 37:5–8). A general obeisance of man to man is mentioned in Proverbs 14:19, as the evil bowing down in the presence of the good. The meaning is to be brought low in the sense of being humbled, or to have one's arrogance knocked out of him.

The most prominent Greek word for *worship* in the New Testament is *proskuneo* and is used sixty times. According to Arndt and Gingrich, this word was used to designate the custom of prostrating oneself before a person and kissing his feet, the hem of his garment, the ground, etc.[2] Strong adds that it is akin to a dog's affectionate licking of his master's hand.[3] This is the word describing the actions of the wise men at Jesus' birth in Matthew 2:2. The word used in John 4:23, where Jesus said, "for the Father seeketh such to worship him," is the same word used in Revelation 7:11 to describe the actions of the angels and elders before God, when they "fell before the throne on their faces, and worshipped God."

Biblical Worship or Dictionary Worship?

The English word *worship* is wonderfully expressive of the act that it describes; however, due to the cultural differences between England when our King James Version was penned and America today, the original words need to be revisited. Stopping one's study at the English word is the primary reason God's people do not understand true biblical worship. The English term comes from the Anglo-Saxon *weorthscipe* (later modified to *worthship* and finally to *worship*) which means "to attribute worth to something or someone."[4] The English definition of worship may be correct in its purpose but not in its practice.

Concerning the difference in the English and the biblical terms, *Baker's Dictionary of Theology* states: "Our English word means 'worthship,' denoting the worthiness of an individual to receive special honor in accordance with that worth. The principal biblical terms, the Hebrew *shachah* and the Greek *proskuneo*, emphasize the act of prostration, the doing of obeisance."[5]

It is no wonder that American Christianity views the act of bowing during worship as unnecessary, different, or overkill. Everything that Americans have heard or read in the English makes little mention of bowing. However, we must ask ourselves, is it really overkill? By whose definition? It would seem only right for the One we worship to define worship—and He has, many times over.

The earlier definitions dealing with the etymology of the word *worship* in Hebrew, Greek, and English are not mine but are offered as documented. Definitions of the word *worship* in Hebrew and Greek are dealt with in much greater detail than in English, and it is these definitions that should frame our thinking. Our Old Testament is a Hebrew book, and the New Testament is a Greek book. I have heard many times from missionaries and language professors that people think in word pictures. Therefore, until we have a grasp of a foreign language and can visualize its distinct word pictures, we cannot understand the thinking of those people. The Old Testament clearly indicates that bowing was extremely important. And for a good while, the Old Testament was the only Bible available to New Testament Christians.

Sometimes it helps to define what a word does *not* mean. If that is true of other words, it is also true of the word translated *worship*, especially if we are looking to the original word(s) for clarity. At the expense of being redundant, let me emphasize that these comments are specifically about the etymology of the word as originally given in its original language. For a moment, resist the tendency to read back into the word your own personal idea of worship. So, what does the word *worship* not mean?

First of all, it does not primarily mean to sit reverently in your pew, although that is admirable. Reverence of any kind is getting hard to come by in entertainment-oriented churches. It does not mean primarily to just bow your head, although bowing one's head could be part of the worship experience. It does not primarily mean to come forward and pray. Prayer can be part of worship, but if it is confined to asking, it may not be worshipping. Simply speaking, prayer is mostly asking God to do something for you, another person, or for His great work. All of this is good and isn't practiced enough, but it may still fall short of what the word *worship* entails. It does not primarily mean to stand and raise your hands toward God. That more closely aligns with praise, which is most excellent and attributes worth to God. Prayer, praise, and worship overlap or blend, but they have their unique distinctions as well.

The fact that so few Christians kneel in worship on Sunday during a service labeled as such suggests a lack of understanding of the primary application of the word. And possibly, it is not so much a lack of understanding as it is a lack of accepting and exercising this understanding. Or, like so many other Bible truths, there is a breakdown between knowing the truth and practicing the truth. At the risk of sounding offensive, worship means to get on one's face, and this can be an unpopular image.

I personally felt shame that I could pastor a church for sixteen years, yet my idea of worship was so insipid. The period of time designated as the worship service included praying, singing, and preaching. These all contained an element of worship but fell short of the primary meaning, which deals with a bowing of the knee, a physical form of humbling, done in spirit and in truth. While we are discussing the word *humbling*, it is a downright embarrassment to me that Satan had a very clear understanding of worship while this preacher did not. Listen to his words to the Savior in Matthew 4:9: "All these things will I give thee, if thou wilt *fall down and worship* me" (italics mine). Be sure to note the *fall down* aspect that Satan understood and demanded. No, the word *worship* is not always prefaced with *fall down*, but the bowing is inherent in the etymology of the word. Shall we do less for our Savior than what those who worship Satan are required to do?

Check it for yourself!

Strong's Exhaustive Concordance of the Bible has long been the standard in pastors' studies, as well as in the homes of serious Bible students. I bought mine while serving on a submarine based out of Charleston, South Carolina, in the early 1960s. I still have it and treasure it for the help I receive in locating verses for particular subjects and original word definitions. However, I must admit that the *Strong's* app on my smartphone has taken over, for two reasons: it is miniscule in size compared to the size of the concordance, and it is much faster. I use it quite often. If you are serious about being fair with the subject of worship, pull up the word on your *Strong's* app and be ready for a treasure trove of references for the Hebrew and Greek word definitions. If you so choose, count the number of times the words *bow*, *humble*, and *prostrate* are mentioned. What percentage of the total word count of worship includes one of those words? How many worship services have you attended in your lifetime? What percentage of the time did you bow? I personally had some catching up to do, and it has been one of my greatest joys.

Chapter Four
The Attitude of Worship

Some works I have read on the topic of worship, by authors whom I respect, mention very little about the physical bowing aspect of worship. That, coupled with the many conversations I have had with pastors, leads me to believe that some pastors are uneasy about suggesting a physical act of bowing. I can understand that since it would be something new and even unusual for most modern congregations. However, how can we bemoan the "seeker-sensitive" entertainment emphasis in other churches, when we are reluctant to suggest a genuine Savior-sensitive atmosphere in our own churches? A real worship event, accompanied by bowing together before God, is given little to no place in our services. Without doubt, a time of genuine worship as part of the worship service would distance us from the entertainment fad and be more biblical at the same time.

I have read some well-meaning writers who literally disannul the bowing aspect in favor of an emphasis on worshipping "in spirit and in truth." I find that emphasis to be out of balance and difficult to accept. To promote bowing while disannulling the spirit-and-truth aspect would be a sham. However, one, without the other falls short of true worship. Bowing was practiced in the Old Testament, the Gospels, and Revelation. Why should our age be exempt? How can we ethically or academically rob a word of its primary meaning? This is a prominent word mentioned well over 200 times in the Old and New Testaments. It cannot be treated as one of those "once used" words with a narrow nail on which to hang its claim. It is, rather, one of the more redundant words in Scripture, giving us plenary support for its meaning.

Interestingly, there is some support here from the secular world. Based on their preliminary findings, published in the journal entitled *Psychological Science*, researchers are now looking at factors that modulate the effect of awe on belief in the supernatural. For example, they are testing whether or not adopting submissive body postures, which make us feel less powerful, might dispose us to experiences of awe. Dr. Piercarlo Valdesolo said such a link could perhaps explain the presence of such postures in religious practice, such as kneeling, bowing, and gazing up. He added, "The more submissive we act, the more awe we might feel, and perhaps the stronger our beliefs become."[1] What should we do if secular experts end up discovering that bowing in a religious practice increases awe, but those who already possessed strong biblical evidence for it have overlooked it?

A number of years ago, our chorale sang a song entitled "O Purify My Life," arranged by Don Marsh, based on David's prayer in Psalm 51. On one occasion, they sang it while kneeling, but only that once. I later asked one of the men about that occasion and why they never sang it again while kneeling. I offer his response as relayed to me: "It was definitely a spiritual experience as well as an emotional one. Speaking for myself, when I sing, my effort and my prayer is to sing not just the words and notes, but also the message. This song, being written and sung in the first person, is easy for me to personalize. It became a prayer, which then became stuck in my throat. I wanted the words and notes to come forth, but I choked up because of the message of how my devotion compared to the love my Savior has for me. There is a certain level of performance required on a platform in front of people, so the difficulty for me was the balance of personalizing the message yet presenting it in an acceptable manner to the congregation." Though not intended to be a worship time, the bowing added that effect to those singing.

In addition to this, the words *spirit* and *truth*, though very important, are not inherent in the word *worship*, as bowing is. Are they suggested in the use of the word? Absolutely, and it is clearly taught in the context of John 4:23. For the moment, however, we are endeavoring to allow the word *worship* to speak for itself. If the truth be known, we are not facing a lack of good academics in our etymology. We are facing a group of Christians who have not delved into the meaning of the word. I was one of those people for a good number of years. I was embarrassed, but I do not wish that on anyone else. On the other hand, the attitude of our culture seems to generate an aversion to the act of kneeling. Disrespect is the order of the day in our country. However, when we observe the Eastern worshippers, especially Muslims, the aspect of kneeling, bowing, or prostrating is unmistakable. It is the primary image portrayed.

The necessity of spirit and truth in the worship experience is native or indigenous to the act of worship. However, the practices of culture can add to or detract from our understanding of the word. The Hebrew culture had no problem with bowing or kneeling, even before each other. In Genesis 18:2, Abraham bowed before his three visitors; in Numbers 22:31, Balaam "fell flat on his face" before the angel of the Lord; in I Kings 1:23, Nathan bowed before King David; and in II Kings 2:15, the young prophets bowed before Elisha.

The Old Testament is rife with these occurrences, but in our modern American culture, to whom do we bow? No one! If we are ushered into the presence of the most powerful individual in our country, our president, we do not bow! Rather, we shake hands!

It should be easy to see how we have missed this great truth of honoring God. It is interesting to take note of who and what sort of person brought up the subject of worship in John 4:23 and 24. Erwin W. Lutzer had this sort of person in mind when he said, "God is looking for worshippers. And, if the religious elite are too proud or too busy to learn to worship Him, He seeks the worship of those whose lives are trapped in moral ruin."[2] Such was the case of the woman that Jesus met at the well. This was the occasion of the very text where He expressed His personal desire for worship.

God literally defines Himself as a Spirit, and Jesus made it plain that He was the Truth. I have no doubt that some may bow during the worship time and yet not do so in spirit and in truth. That is not right. Also, there will be many who sit in their pew, not physically bowing, yet with an attitude of spirit and truth. That is not right, either. If worship is your goal, and if you are capable of physically bowing (some are not), do so. Even with some understanding of the need to bow, most don't. Why is that so? Who can say? Only God knows, but it may be because the spirit and truth element can take place *without drawing attention to oneself*, which makes many uncomfortable. *Bowing and kneeling cannot—they certainly will draw attention.* The intent of John 4:23 and 24 might be more clearly served in our churches today if translated as follows: "God is a Spirit and they that bow before Him must bow in spirit and truth." The problem is not in the translation. The problem lies in the understanding of the word *worship*—by Americans, who have a president, and by the British, who at that time had a king. There is a spiritual element of worship not adequately served by the word *bow*. There is also a physical element not adequately served by an absence of bowing during worship.

You will recall that Strong defines the word translated *worship* to kiss, like a dog licking his master's hand; to fawn or crouch to; to literally or figuratively prostrate oneself in homage; to do reverence to; to adore. H. H. Rowley said, "The first element in worship is adoration."[3]

I suppose most of us have had a dog at some point in time. As a young boy just after the close of World War II, I treasured our family dog, Bozo. I was an only child, and my family was very poor. There was no abundance of toys, like children enjoy today. That dog was my lifesaver from loneliness and boredom. Though only a dog, he provided a form of fellowship. He couldn't talk, but he communicated with body language: the wagging of his tail, the posture of his body, and, most of all, his eyes. I can remember coming out of the house and sitting on the edge of the porch. Bozo was often on the porch, lying down, maybe ten or fifteen feet away. Immediately, when I came out, he would take notice. As I sat there, he would always make eye contact with me, and then, with his eyes fixed on mine and without standing up, he would inch his way toward me. I liked that, and I think, somehow, he knew that I did. When he was finally close enough to touch, his eyes seemed to exude an adoration that only a dog and his master can appreciate. The communication in that act defied the words of a young boy and still defies explanation.

There is a reason that people are attached to their dogs and spend considerable money on them. Dogs can be helpful to people, maybe more so than any other animal. However, that probably isn't the reason so many people have them and spend so much money on them. Most dogs are not service dogs. They are what we call pets. I submit to you that their primary worth to most people is the love they generate in their masters through their adoration. Without abusing the word, let me venture to say, it is the dog's worship of his master, as best he can give it, that endears the dog to the person. I suppose there wasn't anything I would not have done for my dog, just because of his attachment to me. And when he barked, I usually looked to see what was going on. Obviously, he had my ear.

During that same era, when I was a young boy, there were RCA Victor records with the image of a dog on the label of the record, sitting before a gramophone. He had his head cocked, peering into the gramophone with an expression of keen interest. That painting, with the caption, "His Master's Voice," stuck in my mind. The idea was conceived in the 1890s as the title for Francis Barraud's painting of a dog named Nipper, listening to a wind-up gramophone.

In the original painting, the dog was listening to a cylinder phonograph. According to contemporary Gramophone Company publicity material, the dog, a terrier named Nipper, had originally belonged to Barraud's brother, Mark. When Mark Barraud died, Francis inherited Nipper. He also inherited a cylinder phonograph and recordings of Mark's voice. When he played the recording of Mark's voice on the phonograph, Francis noted the peculiar interest the dog took in the recording. He then conceived the idea of committing the scene to canvas. I love it still today and contemplate whether or not Nipper was more attuned to his deceased master's voice than I am to my living Master's voice. I also ponder whether or not my dog Bozo, in his own way, was somehow able to illustrate an attitude of worship.

It may be that in Bible times, when there was less urgency, less clamoring, and less secularism, God's people clearly heard their Master's voice. Like Nipper, perhaps they were more enthralled by it than many Christians are today. God had their full attention, and it was evidenced by their body language, which is touted as stronger than verbal language. H.H. Rowley said, "The Hebrews expressed this by their posture and not alone by their word. For, they prostrated themselves before God. 'O come, let us worship and bow down: let us kneel before the LORD our maker' (Ps. 95:6). They did not come with an easy familiarity into the presence of God. They were aware of his greatness and majesty, and came with a sense of privilege to His house."[4]

It would be difficult for me to exaggerate my benefit from reading a considerable number of books on worship. Those books are what I call keepers; that is, they have a permanent place on the shelves of my library. I am also aware that there are numerous books on the subject that I have not read. Nevertheless, I confess to placing a greater emphasis on the physical act of bowing than most I have read thus far. I have previously stated that I clearly understand that worship involves more than bowing the knee, but I fail to see good reason in the Bible not to bow the knee. I rather see that omission as an exception. I don't know that Napoleon Bonaparte was a particularly spiritual man, but his comments about worship make me reconsider my own spirituality. He said, "If Socrates would enter the room, we should rise and do him honor. But if Jesus Christ came into the room, we should fall down on our knees and worship Him."[5]

Since the idea of bowing is inherent in the translation of the word *worship*, there should be no need for additional encouragement. However, an abundance of illustrations suggests we may need even more coaxing in this area. Some texts suggest that bowing is sort of a litmus test for worship. When Elijah was in duress, thinking he was the only one who was keeping the faith, God told him there were 7,000 who had not bowed their knee (worshipped) to Baal. In Daniel 3:6, the command was: "And whoso falleth not down and worshippeth shall the same hour be cast into the midst of a burning fiery furnace." Even when the bowing is not before God, it is the single element that seems to make or break the act. Esther 3:2 says: "And all the king's servants, that were in the king's gate, bowed, and reverenced Haman: for the king had so commanded concerning him. But Mordecai bowed not, nor did him reverence." In verse 5, it says Haman was full of wrath because Mordecai did not bow or show him reverence. The simple act of bowing was—and remains today—big stuff.

Chapter Five

Elements and Uniqueness of Worship

My wife and I have traveled thirty to forty weeks a year and have usually been in a different church each week since 2003. In addition, we often pick up local religious services on television in motels while traveling. Therefore, it is not unusual for us to participate in or view fifty or more Sunday morning services a year.

Since worship has come to be so meaningful, my ears are attuned to its every mention. Many times I have heard this expression: "We are glad you have come to worship with us today." I love that thought, and at that point, I pay extra close attention to the service as it progresses. I have been most impressed and blessed, at times, with the congregational singing, the preaching service, the invitation, and even a baptism. All of these are blessings to me. They all fit well and contribute to a worship service. However, since the most biblical form of worship is to bow in adoration, I particularly look for that element. Most of the time, it never comes. My heart tells me, for the most part, that God's people have not intentionally avoided that intensely personal time with the Lord; they just have run right past it. Their hearts have been lifted by the sum of the service, and that was considered satisfactory.

It has been said, "The good is the enemy of the best."[1] In the average service designated the worship service, various elements such as fellowship, singing, and preaching may be allowed to become the enemy of worship. Please keep in mind, I am not suggesting that every service be labeled a worship service. The Sunday morning preaching time deserves a prominent place. It is a priority in almost every church I have ever been in, but just think of it—wouldn't it be sad if no preaching took place in a preaching service?

Wednesday nights are often called prayer and Bible study times, and worship need not be emphasized then. It would seem strange, though, if there were no prayer or Bible study. Some might even say that they were in an attitude of prayer, Bible study, or preaching. That isn't wrong, but without actual prayer or Bible study or preaching, isn't more being promised than is being delivered? And if it is fair to expect preaching at a preaching service, or prayer at a prayer meeting, is it not fair to expect worship in a worship service? If you give this comparison equal consideration, you will be hard-pressed not to say that worship is being cut short.

Comparisons are more easily made when objects are placed side by side, so let us compare prayer, praise, and worship. Prayer and praise are definitely elements of worship. Like man, who is body, soul, and spirit (I Thess. 5:23), the three (prayer, praise, and worship) work together, but they each have a particular function. I emphasize again that there should be no hard boundaries drawn between the three. Prayer, praise, and worship remain close friends and definitely overlap, but they each have a particular contribution to make.

Prayer — Asking

Alfred P. Gibbs said it well in his book entitled *Worship: The Christian's Highest Occupation.* "Broadly speaking, prayer is the occupation of the soul with its *needs*. Praise is the occupation of the soul with its *blessings*. Worship is the occupation of the soul with God *Himself.*"[2]

There are many true-to-life stories that illustrate the similarities and differences in prayer, praise, and worship. Just recently, I read of a fireman accompanying a young lady to her graduation from high school. This was an individual whom he had actually rescued from a fire when she was a small girl. During that crisis, her cries of fear and need for help were akin to prayer. They formed a very urgent request! When she was safe and the ordeal was behind her, she expressed her appreciation for his act of bravery in saving her. As time passed, her desire progressed to a feeling of respect and awe. She did not need to be saved again—thankfulness and appreciation had been expressed—but it was the person, and who and what he was, that remained in her mind. Graduation occurred many years after that epic event in her life, but the man who saved her had not been forgotten. He was bigger than life and more special than ever to her on graduation day.

In I Chronicles 4:10, Jabez prayed to the God of Israel, and said, "Oh that thou wouldest bless me indeed, and enlarge my coast, and that thine hand might be with me, and that thou wouldest keep me from evil, that it may not grieve me! And God granted him that which he requested."

In II Chronicles 6:12–42, Solomon knelt before the Lord on a brazen scaffold in the presence of Israel at the dedication of the temple he had built. The overlap of praise and worship on prayer is clear in the beginning of his dialogue. After acknowledging God's person in worship and praising Him for

His goodness to his father David, Solomon moves on to his list of requests. He asks God to hear his prayer as God has heard his father David's prayer. He then asks that God would hear His people's prayer for repentance, for deliverance when facing the enemy, for rain in time of famine, for deliverance from pestilence, for recognition of the stranger who comes their way, and for help when Israel would sin and would be taken captive, if they repented.

One of the most succinct prayers in Scripture is that of Elijah, as recorded in James 5:17–18. It reads, "Elias was a man subject to like passions as we are, and he prayed earnestly that it might not rain: and it rained not on the earth by the space of three years and six months. And he prayed again, and the heaven gave rain, and the earth brought forth her fruit."

Matthew 7:7 says, "Ask, and it shall be given you; seek, and ye shall find; knock, and it shall be opened unto you." James 4:2 says, "Ye have not, because ye ask not." Prayer certainly can be more than asking, but it primarily is a request.

Praise — Thanksgiving

Praise, like worship, attributes worth to God. However, praise may be more expressive of what God has done—His blessings—rather than who He is. For instance, consider Judges 5:2, which says, "Praise ye the LORD for the avenging of Israel, when the people willingly offered themselves." Admittedly, it is difficult to separate God's person from His works, but it is that nuance that gives us another glimpse of how we can honor Him. I Chronicles 16:35 expresses the progression from prayer to praise. "And say ye, Save us, O God of our salvation, and gather us together, and deliver us from the heathen, that we may give thanks to thy holy name, and glory in thy praise." Thanksgiving, in its various forms, and praise are often found in the same verse. "Now therefore, our God, we thank thee, and praise thy glorious name" (I Chron. 29:13). Over and over, the idea of praise is linked to thanksgiving.

This kinship is also corroborated by the etymology of the original words translated *praise*. The primary Hebrew word translated *praise* is *halal*, which connotes "being sincerely and deeply thankful for and/or satisfied in lauding a superior quality(ies) or great, great act(s) of the object." A synonym for *halal* is *yada*, which means to "acknowledge or confess sin, God's character and works, or man's character." The manifestation or expression of these words and other synonyms is "to praise, give thanks, to sing or shout joyfully."[3]

The Greek word in the New Testament reflects the root meaning of the word as "value," and the one word uniformly used in its various forms is *aineo*. The concept in these words is to give praise to whatever or whomever is worthy of praise. The emphasis is upon man's praise to God, and the frequent use of the name of God is instructive.[4]

The physical posture for praise is not as specifically articulated as it is for worship. Psalm 100:4 says, "Enter into his gates with thanksgiving, and into his courts with praise: be thankful unto him, and bless his name." God literally revels in the praise of His people. Charles Spurgeon said, "We must thank God for the mercies we have, or else we shall not have others."[5]

Romans 1:18–32 is the sad commentary of a civilization that had knowledge of God and His goodness yet could not bring themselves to appreciate it. The moral decline noted in those verses had a starting point, or perhaps it should be called a tipping point. God is longsuffering, but Scripture reveals that He has limits. I am convinced, in this text, that the limit is found in verse 21, which reads, "Because that, when they knew God, they glorified him not as God, neither were thankful; but became vain in their imaginations, and their foolish heart was darkened." They did not give God the glory due Him, and neither were they thankful. Those two conditions are bedfellows. Henry Ward Beecher said, "Pride slays thanksgiving, but an humble mind is the soil out of which thanks naturally grow. A proud man is seldom a grateful man, for he never thinks he gets as much as he deserves."[6]

Thankfulness, like happiness, is mostly a choice. We are creatures of relativity in many ways, foolishly judging our status by the holdings of others. It is true that if we look long enough, we will find others who appear to have more than we have. This results in a loss of happiness for some people because they can only think of having what the other person has. And yet if we keep looking, we may find more people who have less than we have. This attitude of unthankfulness is futile. II Corinthians 10:12 says, "For we dare not make ourselves of the number, or compare ourselves with some that commend themselves: but they measuring themselves by themselves, and comparing themselves among themselves, are not wise."

William Law said, "The greatest saint in the world is not he who prays most or fasts most; it is not he who gives alms, or is most eminent for temperance, chastity or justice. It is he who is most thankful to God, and who has a heart always ready to praise Him."[7] Along this same vein, H.W. Westermeyer noted, "The Pilgrims made seven times more graves than they did huts. No Americans have been more impoverished than those—who, nevertheless, set aside a day for thanksgiving."[8]

Paul reminded Timothy that "godliness with contentment is great gain" (I Tim. 6:6). When people are content, they can be thankful and are thankful. Thankfulness is not just an attitude—it is a great quality in the life of the Christian! Before the birth of Christ, Cicero declared, "A thankful heart is not only the greatest of virtues, but the parent of all other virtues."[9] As noted in the definition, praise can and does assume the posture of applause. How many times has my soul soared like an eagle, simply from hearing the preaching or singing of a great Bible truth. Spontaneously, without any intentional effort, an "Amen!" or "Praise the Lord!" wells up in my heart and often out of my mouth. As defined earlier, praise is to "give thanks, to sing or shout joyfully."

Worship—Adoration and Awe

II Chronicles 9:1–12 gives the account of the Queen of Sheba's visit to verify the incredible report she had heard concerning King Solomon, his wisdom, and his wealth. The text says she came to Jerusalem with a very large company and with hard questions to prove Solomon. It is apparent that she had not believed all she had heard, thinking that there was exaggeration. After she had heard his wisdom and had seen his abundance, along with the way his servants conducted themselves and the way he ascended up into the house of the Lord, "there was no more spirit in her" (vs. 4). Her skepticism gone, she declared, "The one half of the greatness of thy wisdom was not told me: for thou exceedest the fame that I heard" (vs. 6).

If the Queen of Sheba could not visualize the greatness of Solomon, our chance of having even the smallest grasp of who our God is and what our God is like is unlikely. We have much more to go on than she did because our God has provided us with two great books or two great revelations of Himself. There is general revelation, which we normally call nature, and there is special revelation—our Bible. We need not go in search of our God, for He is everywhere.

Psalm 19 is an abbreviated attempt by the Psalmist to put into words his view of God's two great revelations. As with a parable, he begins with the physical, that which can be seen and experienced by all. He reminds us that the heavens declare the glory of God, that they are a witness for God, and that there is no place on earth void of that witness. When I think of how big God is, it is the great mountains and the stars in the sky at night that nearly take my breath away. In contrast, though, when I think of His holiness, His love, His mercy, and His grace, it is His written word that captures my heart.

Too many times, **general** revelation (Creation—book one) is sold short of its due place in light of **special** revelation (the Bible—book two). God is the Author of both, and Jesus preferred parables in His preaching. He used them a lot! If you think about it, all of life is somewhat like a parable. Our two revelations follow that pattern, the first being physical (Creation) and the second being spiritual (Bible). The more I look at each of them, the more I am overcome with their Creator. Immanuel Kant referenced the effect of these two revelations on him: "Two things fill my mind with ever-increasing wonder and awe, the more often and the more intensely the reflection dwells on them: the starry heavens above me and the moral law within me."[10] Kant's wonder and awe are fitting elements in worship.

Chapter Six

Can You Worship Without Bowing?

I mentioned in chapter one that I came to Christ in 1958 and have endeavored to serve and to honor the Lord since that time. I also mentioned that I had pastored the same church for sixteen years before I began a more serious study of worship. Those were wonderful years with many coming to Christ. Service after service seemed to be Spirit-filled, and even now I look back on them with great joy. However, we did not bow during the service for the specific purpose of worshipping.

The question may be raised, then—did none of our actions serve as worship? Did we never worship the Lord all those Sundays for sixteen years? I am convinced that we did worship, but with less than a full understanding. I am also convinced that our Heavenly Father accepted and reveled in our worship.

Just as I enjoyed my relationship with my son when he was a child, the Heavenly Father enjoyed and accepted our worship. But I must quickly add that I enjoy my relationship with my son as a grown man even more. I can discuss so much more with him as an adult than I could when he was a child! I would love him unreservedly, no matter what, but had he not matured, our relationship would have been severely limited. And so it was with our church. As we grew in number, we also grew in understanding, which is as it should be.

Acts 17:30 states, "And the times of this ignorance God winked at; but now commandeth all men every where to repent." The text is not in reference to worship, but it does imply that God expects more when we know more. That is also an expectation of every parent, employer, or leader. We have to be careful not to be satisfied with little growth. In I Corinthians 3:1–3, Paul chides the Corinthians for not learning.

> And I, brethren, could not speak unto you as unto spiritual, but as unto carnal, even as unto babes in Christ. I have fed you with milk, and not with meat: for hitherto ye were not able to bear it, neither yet now are ye able. For ye are yet carnal: for whereas there is among you envying, and strife, and divisions, are ye not carnal, and walk as men?

In an attempt to grow in this area, we need to bear in mind both the nuances and the telling differences in prayer, praise, and worship. Maybe a modern-day parable could help solidify bowing as the "normal" physical form of worship. First, recall that the basic Bible definition of the word *worship* in Hebrew and Greek, mentioned over 200 times, references bowing. Refer back to the opening definition and word study for documentation, if necessary. You will note that I have chosen a very mundane illustration that distinguishes bowing from other forms of worship in the worship service. It can be as simple as a meal at a restaurant. It may take a little imagination, but the point should be clear, and I ask that you bear with me.

You are seated, and after being presented with a menu, you are asked what you would like to drink. The most common response is to say, "Water." Water, of course, is H_2O, which would include ice and steam. The waiter responds with the following offer: "Would you like that as ice or steam? We do not serve it as water." Your mind may lock up momentarily, but it would immediately confirm for you that water is the "normal" form of H_2O. Therefore, you are not the one with the problem! It would be perfectly legitimate for you to ask why they didn't serve water. You would probably be within your bounds to think it was very unusual for them to serve only ice and steam, although those are indeed forms of H_2O, and they definitely make their contribution. Still, water is the "normal" form, just as bowing is the normal biblical form for worship, if the etymology of the word means anything.

"We have ice and we have steam, but we don't have water."

The subtlety of the problem can be seen in substitution. How often is prayer or praise substituted for worship! Many are the times I have heard a pastor or song leader say, "Let us worship the Lord in song, in our giving, in our praise, and in our prayers." I have no problem with worshipping the Lord in any or all of these ways, but what has happened to God's desired, normal form of worship? I beg of you to understand that I am not in any way trying to diminish other forms of contribution to worship. By all means, employ the others, but if there is *always* singing and praying in the worship service, is there not a bias against bowing? Is not the emphasis always lopsided? After all, it isn't singing, giving, praising, or prayer that God seeks in John 4:23–24. It is worship!

In actuality, we already believe (rather strongly, I might add) in using word meanings to determine the physical expressions for a biblical practice. Consider the idea of baptism and why we practice immersion. Among other valid reasons, there are two that seem to be used most consistently in preaching and teaching on the subject. The first is that the definition of the word *baptize* means first and foremost to submerse or dip. The second is that uses of *baptize* in the New Testament usually give us a context, helping us realize what it looked like. One difference between studies of *worship* and *baptize* is that the physical expression of worship is modeled many times more than the expression of baptism. Why do we need so little evidence to dip, but we ignore so much evidence to bow? Who wins an argument of biblical credibility when the Baptist scolds the Catholic for ignoring the clear meaning of the word *baptize* while the Catholic reminds the Baptist that he ignores even clearer evidence for the word *worship*?

In addition to substitution, the frequency of worship or the lack thereof accents the bias. I have heard these excuses given: "We have a special worship service once a year," or once a quarter, or once a month. I have heard the reason for that was to protect it—to keep it from becoming commonplace.

Really? I would ask, how often do you have a song service? How often do you have a preaching service? How often do you pray or take an offering? Why not be concerned that they become commonplace? Does the Bible place as much emphasis on any of those things as it places upon worship? Remember the number of times that worship is mentioned in the Bible. Remember how it states that God seeks it. It is mentioned early in the Bible. It resides all the way through the Scripture, and it is of major significance in Heaven, when even the great work of preaching has ceased (Rev. 7:9–12).

Chapter Seven

The Object of Worship

Where Is God?

Everyone has difficulties with things they do not understand. For me, it is the ever-changing face of electronics. I am amazed at what they can do, but sometimes their complexity causes me to forego their benefits.

It may be that way for some people with worship. The basic idea of worship is very simple: *It is the voluntary humbling of one person, physically and spiritually, to exalt another.* However, if simply attending a preaching service labeled a worship service has been the only worship experience, confusion can be expected.

Other than misunderstanding the most basic of definitions for worship, the next greatest obstacle to worship may be the loss of the object of worship. John 4:1–26 is the defining text on this matter, given by Jesus Himself. It is the familiar account of His encounter with the Samaritan woman at Jacob's well. It did not take this woman long to recognize Jesus as a prophet or someone from God. That led to questions, and they were not questions about trivial subjects. They were questions about worship.

She began by asking Jesus where worship was to take place. In verse 20, she questioned whether worship was to take place where the Samaritans worshipped or in Jerusalem where the Jews worshipped. Read her words in John 4:20: "Our fathers worshipped in this mountain; and ye say, that in Jerusalem is the place where men ought to worship." When it comes to worship, especially corporate worship, the place is important. Doubtless, however, it is not the most important. Jesus sidestepped the location question and went straight to the real issue of what or whom she should worship.

In verse 22, Jesus said "Ye worship **ye know not what**: we know what we worship: for salvation is of the Jews."

The Samaritan woman had good intentions, but those intentions were a major distraction to the real issue. Without question, a great number of churchgoers are in the same boat. They mean well, but they are missing the main point. For instance, it is Sunday, about 9:30 a.m., and you stop for fuel. Another car pulls in, and you notice the man is wearing a suit and tie. His family in the car is dressed nicely, as well. So you greet them, "You folks sure look nice this morning; what is the occasion?" The answer? "We are going to church." That is the admirable and proper place to go on Sunday morning. I have nothing but praise for where they were going. However, isn't that what the Samaritan woman emphasized—the place? It is exactly the same! Let me repeat myself. Where you go to church is definitely important. But even more important is what you do when you get there.

Grammar may help illustrate this truth, as well. If we say, "John hit the ball," we have a subject (John), a verb (hit), and a direct object (ball). How much sense does "John hit" make, without the "ball"? Picture a child running into the house, blurting out, "John hit! John hit! John hit!" We would immediately demand, "What or whom!? What or whom did John hit?" Without the direct object, the sentence is not complete and does not make sense. As a matter of fact, it is confusing and frustrating.

Isn't that where the Samaritan woman was? Is that not where many Christians are today? The importance of the facilities, the Sunday school programs, the nurseries for the kids, the music program, the friendliness of the people and the message of the pastor are all under consideration. Meanwhile, true worship of the true God is rarely mentioned.

Let's rewind the gas station scene with a slight change.

"You folks sure look nice this morning! What is the occasion?"

"We are going to church to meet with God. We are going to worship Him."

Nothing is vague about that. The focus is clear, but the answer would seem strange in our modern time because we are programmed more to a place than to a Person. Mentioning the place would be fine, however, if the right Person were sought and honored during the service.

A number of years ago, a longtime friend rang our doorbell. I opened the door and bid him come in. To my surprise, rather than returning the greeting, he just walked past me and on into our house. He had been there many times before and was quite familiar with the surroundings. He made his way into the kitchen and actually found something to eat and to drink, but he was still not conversing with me. He even joined everyone in the family room and talked with the others while I just watched. He enjoyed one of our recliners for a while and then quietly left, without saying a word.

It was a strange experience. It was as if he were thoroughly familiar with our home, enjoyed being there and enjoyed visiting with everyone, but felt no real need or obligation to converse with me, even though it was my home.

Now, you may be thinking, *That has never happened to me.* Well, it really hasn't happened to me, either. However, it is an analogy that came to my mind as God began to deal with me about corporate worship in our church.

Just think for a moment whether or not you have actually seen something similar happen at someone else's house. I have—many times over, in fact. It happens at God's house on a regular basis. Is it not true that people come to God's house on Sunday morning, are greeted at the door, and walk right in? Are they not familiar with the surroundings and other people there? Do they not enjoy the congregational singing, the choir, and the special music? Do they not enjoy everyone's fellowship, shaking hands with them at the close of the service as they leave to go home? They have benefited from a good lesson in Sunday School and have been well fed from God's Word by the pastor. And yet they have not acknowledged the good man of the house (God) the whole time!

It is as Tozer said, "The modern scientist has lost God among the wonders of His world; we Christians are in real danger of losing God amid the wonders of His Word."[1] The singing and preaching of the Word are intact—even inspiring and challenging. But if it seems strange to visit the house of Hardy without ever speaking to him, what about visiting the house of God without speaking to Him? Without question, prayer would acknowledge His presence, but would it acknowledge His worth—who and what He is—as much as worship? I wonder if our coming to the house of God so many times without acknowledging Him properly suggests to Him that He isn't our primary reason for coming and that our purpose is accomplished without Him?

How is it that we will not put up with incomplete grammar in a sentence, and we think it strange if someone comes to our home and ignores us (when we are of little consequence), yet we think nothing of ignoring the Incomparable One? Who and what God is demand worship. He is the Holy One. It is imperative that we meet with God because the right view of God puts everything into perspective. When Isaiah saw the Lord, as recorded in Isaiah 6:1–8, everything else became a distant second. That vision hit Isaiah like a stroke, and as some commentators suggest, he groveled in the dust of his unworthiness. "Then said I, Woe is me! for I am undone; because I am a man of unclean lips, and I dwell in the midst of a people of unclean lips: for mine eyes have seen the King, the Lord of hosts" (vs. 5).

I cannot help but think that, next to the vision of the Lord, high and lifted up in the Temple, the acclamation of the seraphim in verse 3 caught Isaiah's attention, as well. What did they say? What did they not say? They did not say, "Omniscient, omniscient, omniscient," or, "Omnipotent,

omnipotent, omnipotent," or any of His other unmatched attributes. They cried, "Holy, holy, holy," which defies a complete definition, but combines all His attributes and sets Him apart in a class held only by Him. That is basically what *holy* means. It simply means "other than." I know people say that God is love, and that is true. We could say He is merciful and gracious, which would also be true. However, consider this: If He were not holy, His love would be just like our love. Would that be sufficient for you? Are you ready to stake your soul on man's love? Do you want man's version of mercy and grace, or do you prefer God's? Our God has no peers.

That was not all. Isaiah was not the only one whose demeanor and strength drained from him at the presence of the Holy One. Those magnificent creatures positioned above God's throne were also affected. They each had six wings. Wings can do more than enable flight, but flight is the wings' primary function. I do not know exactly what the seraphim looked like. My understanding is that they exude some combination of fire and gold in appearance. Everything I read about them suggests that they are powerful and majestic. I can only imagine what they must have looked like and sounded like, in full flight. Be that as it may, on that day, they were taken up with the holiness before them. With two wings they covered their faces, with two wings they covered their feet, and with two wings they flew. How did these great creatures, designed to fly on six wings, fly with two wings? "Above it (*the throne*) stood the seraphims: each one had six wings; with twain he covered his face, and with twain he covered his feet, and with twain he did fly" (vs. 2, italics mine).

I was born during World War II, and many were the stories I heard as a boy, due to my dad and uncles all serving in the armed forces. There was one particular saying that grabbed my ear early on—Coming In on a Wing and a Prayer. I heard my mother use it many times. The specific details vary as to when the expression was first used, but I believe it was during the Pacific Theater of World War II, around 1942. From that time, the idea has been used by many. Originally, the word picture was of a plane that was damaged—still flying, but precariously. Films of those times portrayed a multi-engine bomber, maybe four engines, but with two engines on one wing not working, limping back to the airfield.[2]

Living in Waco, Texas, in the 1940s and early 1950s, I would often hear the engines of a great plane. I would begin to search the sky for it. If I were in the house, I would run outside to try to see it. Planes were usually taking off from or landing at James Connally Air Force Base. My favorite was the B-36, with six propeller-driven engines, facing aft. When they came in, they made the venetian blinds vibrate so much they nearly came off the windows of our house. Though only in a few museums now, they still amaze me. I never saw one come in with the engines inoperative on one wing. It sure would have looked different—even disconcerting. It would have indicated a serious problem, a major vulnerability.

That was only partly so with the seraphim. Their flying may have been impaired, but there was absolutely no vulnerability. Their flight, in that manner, was voluntary, and the sight for Isaiah was transforming. One thing you cannot miss in the Isaiah 6 account is that **the seraphim and Isaiah did not casually come into the presence of God** and somehow miss acknowledging His presence. I believe the idea of spirit and truth was embodied by Isaiah and the seraphim, but they were also completely overwhelmed physically. The whole account is about the effects of His manifested presence.

A.W. Tozer reminds us, "The impulse to worship is universal. If there is a race or tribe anywhere in the world that does not worship, it has not been discovered."[3] With that thought in mind, if man misses worshipping God, what does he worship?   G. Campbell Morgan suggests that everyone worships to some degree, whatever the form or fashion. "The most blatant infidel, denying the existence of a Supreme Being, yet worships; and w*here there is no object*, then man *enshrines his own intellect, bows down before that,* declaring that he will receive and yield to the things he can comprehend, thus making his understanding the very deity that receives his worship."[4]

If, when we come to a worship service, we are content just to see fellow believers, are we not flirting with enshrining ourselves? Worship of self is more prevalent than we think. It is the primary indictment of Romans 1:25 in the slippery-slope-syndrome text: "Who changed the truth of God into a lie, and worshipped and served the creature more than the Creator, who is blessed for ever. Amen." Disraeli said, "Man is made to adore and obey but… if you give him nothing to worship, he will fashion his own divinities and find a chieftain in his own passions."[5] The object of true worship is God, and He shares that position with no other. St. Anselm reminds us of our lowly state: "Come now, little man! Flee for a while from your tasks, hide yourself for a little space from the turmoil of your thoughts. For a little while give your time to God, and rest in Him for a little."[6]

No man ever saw the Lord without being affected. How is it that the masses can go to their places of worship as if going to the store? Churches that have entertainment-driven services will have consumers as members rather than disciples. I doubt many of us would want to flaunt our degree of spirituality alongside Isaiah's; but one thing is for sure—Isaiah had God's ear. His iniquity was taken away and his sin purged (Isa. 6:7). When Isaiah saw the vision of the Lord in the Temple, he was locked onto the holy Object of worship—and he never lost that vision. After most of his service as a prophet was behind him, the vision remained. Listen to Isaiah 57:15: "For thus saith the high and lofty One that inhabiteth eternity, whose name is Holy; I dwell in the high and holy place, with him also that is of a contrite and humble spirit, to revive the spirit of the humble, and to revive the heart of the contrite ones."

Chapter Eight
The Law of First Mention

The law of first mention is the rule that when a doctrine or a Bible truth is first mentioned, it is given in the context of its original intent. That foundational truth then sets the parameters for proper interpretation for subsequent uses of the term.

When considering the beginning of worship, it is hard not to contemplate the account of Abel and Cain in Genesis 4:1–8. The bringing of their increase was more akin to worship than prayer or praise, but the word *worship* is not in the text. Therefore, it will not be treated as the law of first mention. The law of first mention must be given to Abraham in Genesis 22:5 when giving instructions to his servants: "Abide ye here with the ass; and I and the lad will go yonder and worship, and come again to you."

First, it should be noted that this account of Abraham and Isaac is similar to a recounting of a test. Genesis 22:1 says, "And it came to pass after these things, that God did tempt Abraham." For current usage, the word *test* might be more descriptive because, according to James 1:13, God does not tempt man to do evil. However, He does test us. He had already tested Abraham in Genesis 12 when He commanded Abraham to leave his country, his kindred, and his father's house. Abraham passed that test, but I would submit to you that this test was far greater for Abraham than leaving family and home for a new land. It was a test of sacrifice of the greatest measure. We, too, when we come to the altar for worship, are saying by our actions: "You are my Sovereign, and all that I have is Thine." For Abraham, that was family, possessions, ability, and reputation. It was all.

Second, it is obvious that worship involves sacrifice. If it is similar to Abraham's, it would be a most difficult sacrifice. Such actions must be carefully aligned with the will of God. Abraham's was specifically prescribed and in keeping with God's eternal purpose. God's response to Abraham's actions confirmed that he was working in tandem with the mind of God.

In Judges 11:30–40, Jephthah made a costly vow, based on zeal for a good cause but in no way as a direct command from the Lord. In his hot pursuit of the Ammonites, he carelessly vowed a vow that if he was victorious over his enemy, then whatsoever greeted him at the door of his house when he returned would be offered as a sacrifice. Indeed, he returned home in victory, but when his daughter, his only child, was the first to come through the door, his victory turned to sorrow. Abraham's offering of his son was in no way like Jephthah's careless vow but was in direct obedience to the Lord's command in Genesis 22:2.

Third, worship involves faith. Even though God specifically stated that Abraham was to offer his son as a sacrifice, Abraham still told his servants that he *and his son* would return to them. There isn't even a hint of additional information that would have suggested that Abraham knew how this sacrificial scene was to play out. Here, in this story, is the epitome of Hebrews 11:1: "Now faith is the substance of things hoped for, the evidence of things not seen." In fact, the writer of Hebrews gives ample space to Abraham and his wife Sarah as living examples of faith. They weren't perfect specimens, yet God accepted their faith, and that should give us hope as well. How often do we pray the prayer of the man in Mark 9:24, "Lord, I believe; help thou mine unbelief"?

During the same time frame that God was dealing with me about worship, I had occasion to be immersed in Matthew 7:7–12. How can the child of God not take note of the ask, seek, and knock sequence in that text? I love that text, but God used it to make it painfully clear that my faith was small and, to a degree, misplaced. The Christian faith must have an object of trust— someone in whom faith can be based. That Someone is God. Hebrews 11:6 reminds us that "he that cometh to God must believe that **he is**, and that he is a rewarder of them that diligently seek him." While reading and thinking, I began to visualize my relationship with my son and how much I loved him. I also thought about my dad, who had just passed away a few years before.

My father grew up in the Great Depression and only had the opportunity to make it through the third grade before going to work. He served in World War II and, due to his limited education, had to work physically demanding jobs all his life. I am not sure how he did it, but he made sure that my mother and his two children's needs were met. I cannot think of one thing that my dad would not have given me if he could have. I identified with that and wanted to do all I could for my own son.

While that very thought was in my mind, God clearly communicated to me that I had more faith in my earthly father than I had in Him. He further reminded me that I had more faith in myself to care for my own son than I had in Him to care for me. I remember still, hanging my head in shame and feeling the tears well up in my eyes. I slipped out of my chair, onto my knees, and then fell prostrate on the floor. God had *never* one time failed me, and, even during that shameful moment, I felt His love so real around me. I repented, and then I worshipped.

Fourth, there is the element of fear. Abraham stood, looking down at his son on the altar, with the knife in his hand. The tenseness of the moment and the struggle going on inside Abraham were paralyzing. The command of his God drove him forward, but the love for his son could not be dismissed. He groaned from the innermost parts of his being. Faith was all he had at this moment to help him—or was it? No, it was not! There was also a godly fear. While his arm was outstretched, flexed, and maybe on its way down, how sweet to his ears was the clear voice of God, saying, "Abraham, Abraham … Lay not thine hand upon the lad, neither do thou any thing unto him: for now I know that thou **fearest** God, seeing thou hast not withheld thy son, thine only son from me" (Gen. 22:11–12). I cannot process the idea that Abraham's fear was a slavish fear, but rather one of awe and reverence. It was the normal response of a finite man before an infinite God—a God of overwhelming power, but also of boundless love.

Great is the number of His servants, who have been well served by godly fear. In Hebrews 11:7, we read, "By faith Noah, being warned of God of things not seen as yet, moved with fear, prepared an ark to the saving of his house; by the which he condemned the world, and became heir of the righteousness which is by faith." The first verse in the book of Job describes him as a man who "was perfect and upright, and one that feared God, and eschewed evil." Psalm 103:11 says, "Great is his mercy toward them that fear him."

C. S. Lewis, in his work entitled *The Lion, the Witch, and the Wardrobe*, illustrates this healthy fear through the person of Aslan, the lion who represents Christ. In one scene, there is a conversation among Susan, Lucy, and two beavers, about Aslan.

> "Is he a man?" asked Lucy.
>
> "Aslan a man!" said Mr. Beaver sternly. "Certainly not. I tell you, he is King of the wood and the Son of the great Emperor-Beyond-the-Sea. Don't you know who is the King of the Beasts? Aslan is a lion—the Lion, the Great Lion."
>
> "Ooh!" said Susan, "I'd thought he was a man. Is he— quite safe? I shall feel rather nervous about meeting a lion."
>
> "That you will, dearie, and no mistake," said Mrs. Beaver. "If there's anyone who can appear before Aslan without their knees knocking, they're either braver than most or else just silly."

"Then he isn't safe?" said Lucy.

"Safe!" said Mr. Beaver. "Don't you hear what Mrs. Beaver tells you? Who said anything about safe? 'Course he isn't safe. But he's good. He's the King, I tell you."[1]

As with Lucy, godly fear can be looked upon as a negative, but the Bible does not espouse that position. The Bible discourages the fear of man but not the fear of God. Proverbs 9:10 says, "The fear of the LORD is the beginning of wisdom: and the knowledge of the holy is understanding." Ecclesiastes 12:13 emphatically states, "Let us hear the conclusion of the whole matter: Fear God, and keep his commandments: for this is the whole duty of man." The fear of the Lord is an oft-repeated theme in the Word of God. Matthew 28:8 describes a unique mixture of *fear* and *great joy* that sounds similar to Mr. Beaver's comments to Lucy. Only a healthy fear of God could generate a combination of fear and great joy. The most moving part of the account is when the whole camp bows before Aslan. When Mary Magdalene and the other Mary came to the sepulchre early in the morning, they were greeted by an angel who informed them that Jesus was risen and that they should go and tell His disciples. "And they departed quickly from the sepulchre with *fear* and *great joy*; and did run to bring his disciples word" (italics mine). I absolutely love that! We may not normally associate fear and joy together, but they are in the Word of God. The fear of God is good because He is good. In fact, godly fear offers an incredible number of benefits for the believer.

Job was mentioned earlier as one who feared God (Job 1:1). Note that when all he had—his oxen, asses, sheep (some 11,500 animals), sons, and daughters—were lost, he worshipped. "Then Job arose, and rent his mantle, and shaved his head, and fell down upon the ground, and worshipped" (vs. 20). However, during all his calamity, he had God's ear. When the time was right, the Bible says, "the LORD gave Job twice as much as he had before" (Job 42:10).

Chapter Nine

Personal Worship

Before we leave Abraham and our study of first mention, we must particularly give him credit for setting a compelling example for *individual* and *domestic* worship. That appears to be the right order. God began with individuals, and the first form of worship was individual, personal, intimate worship. Corporate worship began with the institution of the family and then the church. If worship is not part of the individual Christian's life, it may not be in the home. If true worship is not established in the home, it is very unlikely to be found in the church. For a great number of years, individual and domestic worship was the norm for Israel. It effectively set the stage for worship later in the church.

Since the church existed before any of us was born, and considering the lack of spiritual leadership at home for many, the church vies for first place. The church is referred to as "the pillar and ground of the truth" in I Timothy 3:15. That statement suggests that, of all places, we should expect to learn Bible truth at church. I wholeheartedly agree with that concept and cannot imagine how spiritually destitute my childhood and teen years would have been without the truths I learned at church. However, I am uncertain as to whether or not I would have ever been in church if I had not been taken to church on a regular basis. Thus, faithful church attendance and worship at church often depend upon the church's importance in parents' minds. The family is God's basic unit of society, and its importance would be difficult to overestimate. Pastors, missionaries, evangelists, and other full-time workers may be trained and sent out by the church, but they come from the home.

There was no church, synagogue, or tabernacle in the Old Testament when worship emerged. Of necessity, it had to begin with the individual and probably at home. Early in my Christian life, I knelt by my bed every night and prayed. I did not understand the concept of worship academically, but I knelt in reverence to Him, rather than sitting or standing. Therefore, in retrospect, that had to be my earliest expression of worship—and it was at home.

I also vividly remember my first night in a Navy barracks in San Diego, California. There were eighty of us in one long open area. That first night, I was so tired that I just jumped into my bunk. Then I remembered I had not prayed, and something I had never before experienced grabbed me—the fear of rejection. There was an incredible battle going on inside me about kneeling by my bunk as I had at home! What was this battle? I wanted to be accepted by those seventy-nine other men, my peers. Kneeling by my bunk would mark me. It wasn't that I had decided to sow the wild oats of my youth. I was still determined to do right, by God's grace, while in the military. But that first night was tough. I could hear the Lord talking to my heart. "David, are you going to kneel to Me before all these men tonight? Are you?" I did. However, I have to admit, with shame, that it was a struggle for me. As I look back now, I believe the battle for bowing publically before the Lord was won that night when I was seventeen. Have you ever had a battle like that? Some have told me of battles over just bowing their heads and praying over a meal in public. It can be a very real struggle.

For a number of years now, my personal worship has primarily been in my office. That has not been particularly by design but by occasion and atmosphere. My normal fare early in the morning is to enjoy a cup of coffee while reading my Bible. After that, I find myself kneeling with my face buried in my hands in the seat of my chair. At times, I feel inclined to lie prostrate on the floor before Him. My heart is always made glad in either position. It would be hard for me to process the idea of making much of corporate worship on Sunday and being void of it during the week at home.

In addition, oftentimes when I am driving or flying on a plane to a meeting, my heart is inclined to worship. I am not praying or asking for anything, nor am I feeling a particular need to praise, but my mind is just taken up with thinking about Him, who and what He is, and just being quiet and still before Him. I cannot bow during those times, though I prefer to, but there is definitely a connection with my Maker. None of my comments about bowing is meant to take away from these intensely personal times. But for me, these special times alone with Him keep me in tune and somehow build toward corporate worship with my eternal family on Sunday.

Chapter Ten
Worship and Grace

The fact that we cannot do God's work without God's grace should be a self-evident truth to the mature Christian. The first mention of God's grace is in Genesis 6:8, which says, "But Noah found grace in the eyes of the LORD." That happened when God was preparing Noah to build the ark to the saving of his family. From design to physical completion, the ark was far beyond the ability of Noah and his family. Yet it all came together, and his family was saved.

Then, in Exodus 33:12–17, we are given some insight on how Moses became possibly the greatest leader in history. Moses knew God was big enough for the task, but then he questioned God as to how all this would happen. Moses recounts to the Lord that He had previously said to him: "I know thee by name, and thou hast also found grace in my sight" (vs. 12). Moses continues by asking how he will know that he has God's grace, as he begins to relate it to God's presence. By the end of verse 17, it is clear that God's grace is an indication of God's presence. Verse 16 says, "For wherein shall it be known here that I and thy people have found grace in thy sight? is it not in that thou goest with us? so shall we be separated, I and thy people, from all the people that are upon the face of the earth." Moses viewed this grace as imperative to the success of his mission, and, as stated in verse 15, if God's presence (His grace) was not with him, he did not want to go.

Nowhere in Scripture is the importance of God's grace dealt with more fully than in the writings of Paul, and, yea, in Paul's life itself. Paul could be singled out as the **Apostle of Grace**. In I Corinthians 15:10, he said, "By the grace of God I am what I am: and his grace which was bestowed upon me was not in vain; but I laboured more abundantly than they all: yet not I, but the grace of God which was with me." The well-known account of Paul's thorn in the flesh in II Corinthians 12:7–10 provides a concise appraisal of God's grace in Paul's life. He cried out to God to take away his thorn in the flesh. God declined to remove the thorn, but reminded Paul that His grace was sufficient. Sufficient indeed! In the same verse in which God reminded Paul of His grace, Paul made an abrupt about-face with his request. He began to welcome infirmities and literally said that he gloried in them and took pleasure in them.

In II Corinthians 8, Paul illustrated the grace of God on the Macedonian churches that were experiencing hard times. The Corinthian church was not ignorant of their hard times but had failed to see the hand of God through His grace to them. Verse 1 is loaded to the hilt about the presence of grace in the churches of Macedonia. Paul was driven, even obsessed, over the need for the church at Corinth to grasp how the churches in Macedonia were giving above and beyond their abilities, through grace. Evidently the church at Corinth was struggling in that area. Verse 7 suggests that their problem was not a lack of understanding or even of faith but rather a lack of grace. And Paul, maybe more than any other apostle, understood the unfettered reach of grace.

Note the negatives these Christians in Macedonia faced. Verse 2 says they were "in a great trial of affliction," something most of us have never faced. In addition, they were in deep poverty; in contrast, we live in the wealthiest country on earth. However, because of grace, in affliction they had joy! In poverty, they gave liberally! Grace literally reversed the expected consequences of affliction and poverty. Alexander Maclaren was onto something when he gave the working definition of grace as the *motive* and *power* to do God's will, illustrated in nature as the *root* and *product*.[1] Grace has been described by others as the *desire* and *power* to do God's will.

So, what does this have to do with worship? Remember, worship incorporates the element of humility (bowing) and, as such, derives the benefits associated with humility. Being humble leaves some with the feeling of always getting the short end of the stick. This sounds logical and might be true—were it not for God, who is debtor to no one. The great benefit of humility is the added measure of grace. There may be a common grace toward all men, but the scriptures specifically state that God resists the proud and gives grace to the humble (James 4:6, I Peter 5:5). In Romans 5:20, we read, "But where sin abounded, grace did much more abound." Paul reminds us that there is no shortage of grace and even states that, however great sin is, grace excels even more. No matter the odds, grace goes beyond leveling the playing field.

Paul David Tripp, in his book entitled *Dangerous Calling*, has a cautionary section on losing your awe. This chapter follows a number of cautions about familiarity with the things of God and allowing the daily issues of life to move us away from our close unity with Him. Under the six benefits or fruits of a proper awe of God, humility is the first one listed. Real worship will always have an ample portion of awe; and, based on Tripp's linking it to humility, once again grace enters the picture.[2]

Worship certainly is more than humility, but it certainly *is not less.* Humility may not require a direct object, but worship does. Remember our concise and simple definition of worship? *It is the voluntary humbling of one person, physically and spiritually, to exalt another.* It may have an element of abasement, but at the same time it has an element of fulfillment. It almost sounds contradictory, but it is nevertheless true. In Philippians 2:5–11, the Savior humbled Himself in obedience to the death of the cross but was simultaneously highly exalted, with a name above every name.

After preaching on worship at our church and incorporating it into the Sunday morning service, I began to notice an increase in the number of people coming to the altar during the invitation time at the close of our service. Worship time always preceded the preaching. I referenced that increase one time, and later one of our members asked, "Don't you know what is happening? The emphasis on worship, kneeling, and humility has generated a keen interest in the work of God's grace that has come with it. If we are not living up to a Bible truth that has been preached, how will we ever live up to it without more grace?"

The importance of grace and the acquisition of it reminds me of how close and how distant something could be at the same time. While serving in the Navy, it was our family's lot to move whenever new orders came. I never liked moving, and I still don't! One particular aspect that seemed to be a problem every time we moved was the electric receptacle in the laundry room. The plug on our dryer was never the right configuration for the receptacle in the wall. All the power we needed and more was only a fraction of an inch away. It might as well have been a thousand miles away! That is the way it is with grace. It is close, and there is more than enough of it, but the receptacle, according to the Bible, is humility. To refuse to humble ourselves is to forfeit grace and to invite resistance from God. God's response to an individual who humbles himself before Him is amazing.

When young King Josiah was 26 years old, he ordered the house of the Lord to be repaired. During that time, Hilkiah the priest found the book of the law in the house of the Lord. After it was read to the young king, he rent his garments. II Kings 22:8–20 gives the account. In verse 19, God hears and comforts Josiah and says it was because he humbled himself before the Lord.

Maybe even more amazing, at least to this writer, is the account of Ahab in I Kings 21:25–29. This passage plainly states that no one compared to Ahab when it came to wickedness. The word pictures are vivid. Ahab sold himself to work wickedness in the sight of the Lord! He emptied himself—he gave all to it (idolatry, theft, murder, and more), propelled even more by the counsel of Jezebel, his wife. However, even with this sordid record, in verse 29, Ahab humbled himself, and God took note of it, deferring judgment until after Ahab's death. Amazing, absolutely amazing!

While humility alone may not demand a direct object, worship does. When a person humbles himself before a sovereign, you have worship. Bowing before Him speaks volumes. As a young Christian, I benefited so much from godly music. Some songs provide more word pictures than others do; the old hymn, "Kneel at the Cross," not only conveyed a great truth but supplied a graphic image, as well. More recently, I have thoroughly enjoyed the song written by Chris Machen and Mike Harland entitled "Bow the Knee," usually sung as a solo. Seldom have I heard it without being brought to tears.

Chapter Eleven
The Witness of Worship

Growing up in America, one doesn't know much about a monarchy. As a child, all I knew was what I had been told by my mother concerning Old Testament Bible stories and what I had read from storybooks with pictures. Most people back in the early 1950s did not own televisions, but on one occasion I had the opportunity to watch television at another person's house. Since we did not have a television, this was quite an experience for me. The black-and-white picture was not all that great. Nevertheless, I was excited.

The program was about the old country, and presently a group of men dressed in robes emerged from a castle. In my mind, kings lived in castles, but in this picture no one was wearing a crown, which I also associated with kings. *Who is the king?* I wondered. Then a man approaching the group knelt on one knee with his head bowed before one particular man. Immediately, I knew which man was the king! Interestingly, as I think back now, I did not know who the king was by what the king did; I knew who the king was by what his subject did!

Obviously, there are times when kings wear their crowns and regal garments, and no one can be in doubt at that point. However, it is not always so. The Christmas song, "How Should a King Come?," reminds us that our King did not initially come in the expected way, although someday He will. Until that time, like the scene from the old country, it may be up to the King's subjects to ensure that He is recognized and has received His due respect.

Our King may not have castles in our land today, but He does have sanctuaries. However, American Christians seem to adapt quickly to applause and forms of entertainment while exhibiting an aversion to bowing publicly.

In what way, then, is there a witness to our Sovereign? If the Bible words for worship, both Hebrew and Greek, call for a bowing, why is it not happening? Certainly one reason must be that church members still do not grasp that it is the literal meaning. I believe that as pastors we have failed our people and our God in this area. Some pastors may have meant well in being sensitive to how visitors may feel about worship, but clearly the pendulum has swung too far in that direction. The worship of man may not be our intent, but an objective observation of our worship services and to whom they cater may suggest otherwise. I honestly cannot see where the Scriptures give us that license.

In reading through this manuscript, our pastor referenced an occasion that caused him to question whether to have the worship service on a particular Sunday. He said, "I remember after we started the worship time at Bible Baptist that it came time for Bible School Sunday, when we would have 40 to 50 guests, mostly bus parents. I struggled with what to do with our worship time; I came close to the decision to eliminate it during these services with lots of visitors. God dealt with my heart, though, about the fact that it would make a powerful statement for these guests to see us bowing before God. I did not know how they would respond. I've never passed over the bowing time due to visitors, and I've watched the vast majority of them join us. The exceptions have been rare (I can't actually remember one, but I'm sure there are some). That has been a few years ago, and now no one at Bible Baptist considers it strange at all to bow in front of these strangers. I've had nothing but great comments about it, and it has also served as a check for me to avoid being overly seeker-sensitive."

Many times I have seen small decals on the rear windows of cars in front of me. I particularly take note of them when stopped behind one at a traffic light. Sometimes, they portray a mom and dad with a certain number of children, telling you something about their family. Sometimes, a pet may be included with the group. My all-time favorite is a cowboy kneeling before a cross, while his horse stands nearby with his head down. It is an unmistakable icon proclaiming the allegiance of that driver to Christ. How is it that we can understand that, when it appears on the rear window of a car—yet we miss it at church?

For a moment, I ask you to bear with me, as I offer a hypothetical illustration. Let us suppose the earth is visited by aliens from another planet. If they could visit our world, they would be intelligent. Let us also assume they have read our literature. They have learned enough about humans to know we are religious and believe in a higher power. We will further assume that they have acquainted themselves with our theological jargon, which would give them an understanding of worship. They know that the original words mean to bow before their sovereign—their king. Consequently, they visit a Baptist church on Sunday morning during the prescribed time for worship. Whether they peer through the windows or have visible access another way, they watch to see the church members express the worth of their Sovereign. Their next stop is an Islamic mosque. Based on the action of the subjects, both in a Baptist church and in a mosque, which do you think they would decide serves a real sovereign?

The identity of the one true God is certainly the priority, but the identity of the worshipper is important, as well. Reluctance here may reveal a hidden problem as to whether we really want to be identified as servants of Jesus Christ. Maybe that servanthood causes embarrassment for some who bear His name. Because of pending persecution, Paul was concerned about that very possibility in the life of Timothy. He admonished him in II Timothy 1:8 to not be "ashamed" and reiterated his own position, saying, "I am not ashamed," in verse 12. I am afraid that Christianity in America has grown soft, as compared to the faith of our founders in the early years of our great country.

About three years after we instituted a set time at Eastland Baptist Church to worship in our Sunday morning service, a pastor friend from out of town attended, as he was just passing through. I knew he was there but only had time to greet him briefly. A few days later, I received a letter from him, describing the impact the service had upon him. He labored over trying to describe it; he said it was the most worshipful service he had ever attended. The regular morning service had remained intact from the previous years, but a time to kneel before the Lord had been added. When that time came, he noted that the people eagerly and joyfully knelt before the Lord. Kneeling always points toward a sovereign. It is a *witness*.

Maybe to some the idea of worship is but a small matter in the Christian life, but Philip Hughes deals that position a hard blow. "Worship of the true God in spirit and in truth is essential for the integrity of man as a religious being and an indispensable component of the lifeline which connects the spiritual creature to his spiritual Creator, who is the source not only of his existence but also of the harmony and goodness of his existence. For man to turn away from this spiritual communion with his Maker is for him to throw away the key to the understanding of his origin and his destiny."[1]

Chapter Twelve
The Conflict of Culture and Worship

Part of our problem with bowing we have come by honestly. In 1611, when our King James Bible was translated from the original languages, there was no America as we know it. The land was here, but not the great missionary-sending country of America. Additionally, England was different from America. Its leaders were kings and queens. The proper way to approach a sovereign in a monarchy is to bow the knee. That would have been the way King James would have been approached. In a republic, like America, we have no kings or queens; we have presidents, first ladies, vice presidents, and a congress. Though we pay honor to our leaders, we do not bow before them. We shake their hands.

The point is, the people of England, under King James and later, understood the term *worship*. America is familiar with the word but is unfamiliar with its biblical meaning. Our God is not a president voted into office—He is sovereign over all. Therefore, how do we greet Him? Do we bow before Him, as we should, or do we just shake His hand?

Another problem accented by our culture is the casual seeker-friendly attitude that is more aligned with entertainment than with worship. I think almost everyone can sense the pull that casualness has on God's people; and, yes, there is certainly a time and place for it. The child of God has the benefit of enjoying His presence anytime and anyplace. Many are the times when God helps us with mundane tasks when we are far from suits and sanctuaries. I cannot begin to express how thankful I am for that. The whole idea of the Incarnation was so that Christ could identify with us in our everyday lives and the accompanying struggles. This is the reason

He put Himself in a position to be tempted "in all points…as we are, yet without sin" (Heb. 4:15).

Oh, how precious it would be if, like the believers on the road to Emmaus in Luke 24, we could walk with Him in our leisure clothes or work clothes, hear His voice, and glance over at Him from time to time. If you think about it, that **is** how we spend most of our time with Him, if we are so inclined. To think that our great God only meets with us during church services is a travesty of His claim to be with us always. When Paul encouraged the Thessalonians to "pray without ceasing," he was reminding them that God was there and that He was interested in everything they faced.

As I look back over the years of my pilgrimage, some of the greatest times of spiritual growth occurred in what I refer to as *casual* times. One of the benefits of being older is to have a longer span of time to survey how God intervened over and over to accomplish His will in one's life. His sovereign hand is at work every day. As a little boy, I experienced His genius in the design of the home and was mesmerized by the intricacies of His creation. I recall how He guided me through my teen years and the especially challenging times when serving on a submarine, separated from family and friends. Then, through my adult years in college and seminary, guiding a family, fixing cars, repairing a house, etc., I was always looking to God for direction, wisdom, and strength. I still function that way and am most thankful for those times of *casual* fellowship and instruction.

However, let me hasten to another experience I highly treasure—my *formal* time to honor my God. It is then that I see Him in His normal state and am reminded that the *casual* times are times He somehow lowers Himself in order to fellowship with an earthly son or daughter. For some, it may suggest that He is content to be like us and with us, as we are and as the earth is. For many of us, though, that *formal* time is a constant reminder of how far above us He really is and how far He came to take upon Himself the form of a servant for our sake. Yes, His lowering of Himself can but lift Him ever higher in the eyes of the redeemed.

Isn't that what Philippians 2:5–11 is all about?

> Let this mind be in you, which was also in Christ Jesus: Who, being in the form of God, thought it not robbery to be equal with God: But made himself of no reputation, and took upon him the form of a servant, and was made in the likeness of men: And being found in fashion as a man, he humbled himself, and became obedient unto death, even the death of the cross. Wherefore God also hath highly exalted him, and given him a name which is above every name: That at the name of Jesus every knee should bow, of things in heaven, and things in earth, and things under

the earth; And that every tongue should confess that Jesus Christ is Lord, to the glory of God the Father.

Oh, how my soul rejoices and soars when touched by songs like "Be Thou My Vision," by Dallan Forgaill, and "High and Lifted Up," by Dianne Wilkinson. And no, I do not think you **have** to be dressed a particular way or in a certain place and atmosphere to appreciate the fellowship of the Lord. However, I cannot fathom that any blood-bought child of God would not **want** to honor his Lord by being in His sanctuary and presenting himself in his best. How we dress around someone has always made a statement about that person's importance to us. Something is wrong with the attitude that says, "I enjoy the casual times that I have with the Sovereign of all, and I am thankful that He comes down to meet with me, but I am not thankful enough to go out of my way to meet with Him formally." Be sure that Habakkuk didn't think that way, for he wrote, "The Lord is in his holy temple: let all the earth keep silence before him" (2:20). Neither did Isaiah take His presence lightly, when he saw Him in the temple in Isaiah 6. Nor did the Apostle John on the Isle of Patmos in Revelation 1:13–15.

The times of *casual* fellowship and learning far outnumber the *formal* times, and we will rejoice in each one of them. But let us make sure that those *casual* times are not cheapened by our devaluation of the *formal* times, which demonstrate how highly we think of the One Who came so low. It may be that the demise of Cain and his offering, as well as Uzzah's handling of the Ark of God, was steeped in too much *casualness*. Presidents and kings lend themselves to casual relations at sundry times and divers manners, but that is **not** their norm, nor should we wish it to be so. Nay, we wish our King to be high and lifted up, so it is obvious that He has no equal.

The rise of entertainment in the church has made its entrance with the throng of *casualness*. The less we make of God, the more we make of self. Nowhere does the Bible suggest that God needs or desires entertainment. Entertainment is an occupation of the mind—a diversion or amusement. God needs none of this. Therefore, it is void of any spiritual value to the believer when it is introduced into that sacred meeting with God.

Not only has entertainment thrived with casualness, but it has also thrived with pragmatism. Myriads of pastors know the difficulties of starting a new church. The Scriptures make it plain that men **do not** seek God, so the pastor and people must go after them. The alternative is to offer something they **do** seek, which includes entertainment. No one wants to preach to empty pews, and empty pews do not pay the bills. The pressure to incorporate entertainment in order to get a crowd is more than most can resist. Thank God for large churches, for every person is a soul for whom Christ died. However, it is less than honest to suggest that a crowd of people in a building with a steeple constitutes a church. To paraphrase

G. Campbell Morgan, a church is a group of people committed to the lordship of Christ.

The bottom line is this: does the success of a mega-church justify the methods to get there? Does the end justify the means? Yes, this is a worn and weary axiom that is still debated. In the business world, perhaps it should be debated, but in the Lord's work, it is the Lord's call. Let us draw from just two portions of Scripture that will clarify this thought.

First, consider the temptations of Christ in Matthew 4:1–11 and pay special attention to the third temptation. The first two are very important, but it is the third that was the litmus test and most closely aligns with our subject. In verses 8 and 9, the devil shows Jesus all the kingdoms of the world and their glory, and says, "All these things will I give thee, if thou wilt fall down and worship me." It would seem that all the kingdoms of the world, even at that time, would exceed any single gathering of our largest churches today. *The temptation here, as in the first two, was that a divine end should be reached by other than a divine method.* It was a classic example of doing the right thing the wrong way. For Jesus to do that would have been for Him to place the *work of God* above the *person of God*. Frederick Bruner was right when he said, "Only God is God."[1]

Second, Luke 14:25–33 gives a concise and somewhat pungent response of Jesus to the great multitudes that followed Him. Three times He spelled out the requirements for one to be His disciple, and they were everything but entertaining. Family, self, and possessions had to be a very distant second to the Lord Jesus if His followers were to achieve a disciple's status.

Note in this passage the analogies of the tower and the army and the emphasis on counting the cost. It is reminiscent of the great work of Nehemiah as he led the people of Jerusalem to rebuild the wall. Nehemiah 4 gives the account of the people holding either trowels or swords. As they worked at rebuilding the wall, they also had to guard against the enemy. It was a difficult time. Verse 23 gives us some insight as to their dedication by mentioning that they only put off their clothes for washing. They were always ready to build or defend. Based on this dedication, Spurgeon titled his paper *The Sword and the Trowel.* Building and fighting were the issues, and both were expensive.

However, the emphasis on counting the cost in Luke 14 was not for the disciples alone. Jesus was counting the cost, as well. Who was and Who is the Builder of the church and the Warrior of Armageddon? What kind of helpers did He require to build the church? What kind of commitment was needed from those who would serve with Him? Total commitment was essential, enabling them to face overwhelming odds. Jesus confronted them about facing 20,000 with only 10,000 and whether it could be done, or if they would send an ambassador and try to strike some kind of deal. Jesus had no plans to strike any kind of deal, so in light of the picture Jesus painted, the three stringent requirements were a must.

Developing disciples remains a critical issue for pastors today. We can make all the excuses we want about the current culture, but if a church is to be built like Jesus intended, disciples have to be made. Briefly stated, in light of Luke 14, pastors must make disciples, or they will have to make concessions. A church filled with consumers, drawn by entertainment rather than duty, is not the church Jesus built.

As Tozer said, "The church that can't worship must be entertained, and leaders who can't lead a church to worship must provide the entertainment."[2]

Chapter Thirteen
Worship and Revival

America is not going to remain the world leader without revival. I am all for God's people voting, and I certainly would not minimize the great contribution made by godly leadership. However, we all know that our God has been very clear about what needs to happen for a country to see revival. II Chronicles 7:14 identifies the people who can make this happen: it is His people, called by His name! The Pilgrim Fathers understood this clearly—

> Ay, call it holy ground,
>
> The soil where first they trod.
>
> They have left unstained, what there they found---
>
> Freedom to worship God.
>
> —Felicia D. Hemans, *Landing of the Pilgrim Fathers*

Pay special attention to the first thing He says we must do in II Chronicles 7:14. The order here is critical. The first thing is to **humble** ourselves. We are a proud people, maybe because some equate humility with weakness. But humbling oneself is not for the faint-hearted.

Immediately following and closely tied to being humble is **prayer**. Prayer is hard work, and I don't know that I have ever heard any of my acquaintances say that they were as fervent and as effectual in their prayer lives as they should be. It was not that they didn't want to be. It is just hard work for the flesh! Satan is opposed to prayer, and he fights our every attempt. We are no match for Satan; hence, he wins all too often, robbing us of our prayer time.

When we humble ourselves and pray, we are building a momentum to **seek** His face. This is the third command in this verse. Oh, if we could only see Him as He is. Like Moses, who had the desire to see His glory, may we be afforded a glimpse from our cleft in the rock (on our knees in prayer).

Fourth, He said we must **turn** from our wicked ways. How oft, to myself, alone in my car, or walking alone, I have sung, almost never without tears—

> Prone to wander, Lord, I feel it,
>
> Prone to leave the God I love.
>
> —Robert Robinson, 1757, age 22

Remember that primary element of worship involving bowing and humbling. It is the attitude of worship. And remember what God does for the humble—He gives grace. The order of this verse is crucial. It does not say to pray first or to seek His face first or to turn from their wicked ways first. That is because we do not have the ability to do any of that without God's grace. Remember, as was referenced in the chapter on Worship and Grace, the great Scottish preacher, Alexander Maclaren, in his notes on I Corinthians 15:10, referred to grace as the *root* and *product* or *motive* and *power* of Paul's work.[1] Others have defined grace as the *desire* and *power* to do God's will. God's grace was and is absolutely necessary to pray effectually, to seek His face and to turn from our wicked ways. This is God's prescription to have our sins forgiven and see our land healed. It absolutely cannot be done in our own strength.

Knowing that prayer, seeking His face and turning from our wicked ways is a tall order, we cannot help but consider if it even can be done. Should we just throw up our hands in defeat and let come what may? No! More than once I have been asked: "Can America have revival?" I always unequivocally contend that America not only **can** have revival, but that God **desires** that America have revival. The question must be raised then: why don't we desire revival? Some may look back to the days of our great evangelists and try to lay the blame for lack of revival on our current evangelists. That may indeed be **a** problem, but I do not believe it is **the** problem.

Consider the parable of soils in Matthew 13. In that parable, the seed was the Word of God, and Jesus was the preacher. Therefore, there is no fault to be found with either the sermon or the preacher. The variable was with the soil or the hearts of men (vs. 15). The chapter describes the wayside or calloused heart, the stony or shallow heart, the thorny or crowded heart, and last, the good heart. Without question, we preachers have more than enough to answer for concerning the lack of true revival. Yet in glancing back at II Chronicles 7:14, I see that the verse does not place the burden of action on the prophets, but on His people as a whole, which would include the prophets. As with the parable of the soils analogous to the hearts of men, three-fourths of them were not compatible with the Word of God. Therefore, the heart condition appears to be our problem in America.

However, there is reason for hope. Isaiah 57:15 clearly speaks of God's desire for revival: "For thus saith the high and lofty One that inhabiteth eternity, whose name is Holy; I dwell in the high and holy place, with him also that is of a contrite and humble spirit, to **revive** the spirit of the humble, and to **revive** the heart of the contrite ones." God's heart is moved by the humble, and His storehouse of grace is open to them. Before Isaiah linked God's presence with the humble in spirit, Moses had linked God's grace with His presence in Exodus 33:16. Since God resists the proud and gives grace to the humble, the two thoughts are almost synonymous. God's dwelling with us means we have His grace. Conversely, to have God's grace is to have God's presence. It is a wonderful, invaluable, and indispensable truth.

Being finite creatures, we are overwhelmed with the poor spiritual condition of our great country. It is easy to think that she is too far gone and cannot be restored. Sin is rampant and unrestrained. Humanly speaking, she absolutely **is** too far gone, but enter grace! "Where sin abounded, grace did *much more* abound" (Rom. 5:20, italics mine). Did you catch that? When sin is great, God's grace is greater still. God's grace levels the playing field, no matter the magnitude of the sin factor.

I believe God longs for and waits for the opportunity to show Himself great in America. Oh, what would it be like for all the redeemed in America to be on their faces before God? What rejoicing there would be, as He hears, forgives, and heals! I honestly believe that the primary thing standing in our way is the pride factor. It is the worst of all sins because it is the one sin that robs us of the power to conquer the other sins. Pride, the opposite of humility, not only robs us of grace, it also brings resistance from God Himself. How can we have revival when God is working against us as a nation? We must have a humility that opens the door for grace and what more truly sincere humility is there than that enshrouded in worship? No wonder Emerson asked, "And what greater calamity can fall upon a nation than the loss of worship?"[2]

We need a revival of public worship, which in turn may be the beginning of true revival for America, or any other nation for that matter. Only when God's people have a vision of God, like Isaiah did in Isaiah 6, will they have an accurate picture of their own condition and the condition of their nation. We still have it good in America, no doubt; but the constant barrage of bad news describing hostilities, thefts, immorality, indecency and lack of common sense are a drain on God's people. Maybe the Psalmist was experiencing similar conditions in his own country when he wrote, "Wilt thou not revive us again: that thy people may rejoice in thee?" (Ps. 85:6) It may be that we have become so secular that how well we think we are doing is based only on material items. God knows that we need the necessities of life, but He also knows that we often long for more than we need. I Timothy 6:8 says, "And having food and raiment let us be therewith content."

The Old Testament culture was agrarian. I well remember one of my professors saying this about Israel: "As long as the grass was high enough to tickle the cow's belly, they didn't need God." That was true from their point of view because it describes how they felt, but the real truth was that they needed God desperately. If we move forward in time, we eventually arrive at the church age and the Laodicean church of Revelation 3:14–22. They thought that all was well because they were affluent. However, Scripture says, "Thou art wretched, and miserable, and poor, and blind, and naked" (vs. 17). They had totally missed Jesus' earlier warning that "ye cannot serve God and mammon," (money) in Matthew 6:24. The cry of God's people today should reflect the heart of the prophet, as recorded in Habakkuk 3:2b: "O Lord, revive thy work in the midst of the years, in the midst of the years make known; in wrath remember mercy."

What would you be willing to pay for revival? If a financial figure could be placed on it, would you not consider the very most you could give? If it could be bought, I believe a massive amount of money could be raised in our country to bring it about. I believe great sacrifices would be made financially by some of God's people. If revival could be bought, and if revival actually came about, great changes would result. One of those changes would be a revival of awe for our God. And what would we do in return for His great power and outpouring of His Spirit? We would worship.

With that thought in mind, why not turn the order around? If God's granting a revival would bring us to a point of worship, why not humble ourselves before the Lord and gain His matchless grace, which would give us the desire and ability to pray effectually, seek His face, and turn from our wicked ways? According to Isaiah 57:15, it is His desire to revive our hearts and our spirits. Nevertheless, many who know these verses do not humble themselves before the Lord.

For sake of illustration, let me use a personal hypothetical anecdote. I am not a good gift buyer, unless I have prior knowledge of something a person wants. Every birthday and every Christmas, I go through this ordeal, as I try to have attentive ears while the important day approaches. I personally keep a tool catalog and other sources marked with items desirable to me, thus relieving my wife of this conundrum. She does not leave one for me! Even so, let's say, on a certain occasion, I do know what she might like—she wants several rooms of our home repainted! Painting is at the absolute bottom of my list—one of my very least favorite things to do.

In order to head her off, I offer to buy new living room furniture. It doesn't work. She still wants paint! However, I am convinced that my offer was fair, and I am resolved to stand my ground. Now, let me say that my wife is an exceptional woman. We have been married 55 years, and I have been a blessed man because of her. In reality, I could never financially afford to give her what she really deserves. But this time, I am set, and I tell her as much: "I know what you want, but I am telling you what you are going to get!"

How do my statement and accompanying attitude sit with you? You may have words for me, and I would not be surprised. I would have them coming.

We know from Christ's own lips what the Father seeks. It is worship! The word *worship* in that very verse (John 4:23) means to fawn, to crouch, to prostrate oneself as a dog approaches his master and licks his hand. If we are unwilling to give what He desires, especially since it costs not one penny, are we not mimicking my analogy? Do we not say, if only with our actions, or the lack thereof: "I know what you want, but I am telling you what you are going to get!"

I expect you do not like my harshness or my tone, and neither do I. I would never speak to my wife that way. Nor would I ever speak to God that way. However, since body language—our physical actions—is more powerful than the spoken language, I may, in fact, be guilty.

In my heart, I love giving. It brings a special joy. That joy is never greater than when you can find the perfect gift. You can hardly wait to give it! You count the seconds and virtually hold your breath in anticipation of the recipient's response. Such times account for some of the greatest moments of my life.

We know the perfect gift for our Sovereign, and we can all give it. He has placed it within our reach. It is worship, which is *"the voluntary humbling of one person, physically and spiritually, in order to exalt another."*

Before leaving this chapter on worship and revival, let's revisit the idea of worship and the ear of God. Remember the order of II Chronicles 7:14, the great revival verse? It says if God's people are to humble themselves, to pray, to seek His face, and to turn from their wicked ways, there is a wonderful promise. God says, "...then will I **hear** from heaven, and will forgive their sin, and heal their land." The humbling that always comes with biblical worship will gain God's ear.

Chapter Fourteen

A Biblical Format for Worship Services

Church services, as Baptists have known them, are not given in detailed or chronological order in the New Testament. The various elements are taken from a variety of scriptures and combined to make the service as we know it. The most comparable example we have, which closely identifies with Baptist services, is in Nehemiah 8:1–12. The similarities are striking, especially if the style of preaching is expository.

Alexander Whyte, the famed Scottish preacher, saw this comparison with Ezra many years ago. He spoke of such masters of pulpit exposition as Chrysostom, St. Augustine, John Calvin, Matthew Henry, Thomas Goodwin, and Joseph Parker. He then declared:

> All those men laid out their pulpit life on Ezra's exact plan. That is to say, not so much preaching trite and hackneyed texts but reading in the Law of God consecutively, giving the sense, and causing the people to understand the reading. It is a noble tradition and a perfect method; only to do it well demands very hard labor and very wide reading and very deep thinking, as well as an early and a life-long preparation of the preacher's heart. But he who sets to himself this noblest of all possible tasks, and perseveres to the end in it, ever learning in it, ever improving in it, ever adding to his treasures of exposition and illustration, ever putting himself into his lecture, and ever keeping himself out of it, he will never grow old, he will never become worked out, he will never

weary out his people, but he will to old age bring forth his fruit in his season, and his leaf will not wither.[1]

The church service described in Nehemiah 8:1–12 was corporate worship—the people gathered (vs. 1). Remember, however, if there is no private worship, then corporate worship will not enjoy its full potential. Private worship should lead to corporate worship, and the burden of this text lies with corporate worship.

Their worship in this passage was based on God's Word. It is interesting to note that it was the people who asked Ezra to bring the Book. A great revival was in the making, and they somehow knew they needed the Book. It should be noted that this meeting wasn't a seeker-sensitive meeting. It was a God-sensitive meeting. It was content-driven.

The preacher, Ezra, stood on a pulpit of wood in order to be seen and to project his voice. He was accompanied by thirteen additional men (vs. 4).

Evidently, the Book was held in high esteem, for when Ezra opened the Book, all the people stood up. That may suggest that Ezra was aware that he was just a tool and that any special recognition should be directed toward God's Word (vs. 5).

It is in the next verse that we begin to notice a slight difference in the format. Today, everyone is eager to receive a blessing. They go to church anticipating a service designed to accommodate them. In contrast, as this great revival is unfolding, the blessing is directed toward the Lord—not the people (vs. 6).

In addition, it appears the people were spontaneous with their praise when the Word of God was opened and read. They said, "Amen, Amen." After saying, "Amen," they raised their hands. Many have been the occasions in my Christian life that I heard an amen and simultaneously saw a lifted hand, sometimes accompanied by a tearful eye.

Please notice—it was not over yet. There was a progression from Ezra setting the tone by blessing God to pointing the people's attention in the right direction. They then found their own way. They confirmed God's truth by saying, "Amen," raising their hands in praise, and then bowing down with their faces to the ground in worship. Bowing is the most biblical posture for worship.

The preaching service was an integral part of the service that day. Verse eight reads like a homiletic distillation. They read in the law distinctly. There was no hurry here, so the preacher would be able to say something important. The Word was first and foremost. We call that proclamation. Then they gave the sense; in other words, they explained the text. We call that interpretation. Third, they caused the people to understand. We call that application. Alexander Whyte was right. The masters of the pulpit still follow this same format in the preaching service today.

Preachers who still preach to lift up Christ—those who are seekers of the souls of men—are loath to close a service without an invitation. In this account, it appears the people were so moved that they were already repentant, and so much so that they needed some affirmation. That affirmation was given them by Nehemiah, Ezra, and the Levites. They said, in verse 9, "This day is holy unto the LORD your God." In other words, it had been a good day!

The service was closed with a benediction. They were told to go their way and to do that with joy and not with sorrow, for the joy of the Lord was their strength. Verse 12 says they went away with "great mirth, because they had understood the words that were declared unto them."

Note that the format given in Nehemiah 8 does not in any way take away from the preaching, but praise and worship are not neglected. We might be hard-pressed to explain why we have borrowed so much from Nehemiah 8 but yet have chosen to exclude encouraging God's people to worship Him. Is it possible that preachers are more concerned about receiving a spoken "Amen" for what they are doing rather than encouraging adoration and awe toward God for what He has already done? The worship element is not intended to replace the preaching, but neither is the preaching intended to preempt the worship, as it has done in so many churches.

Have Patience and Be Sensitive

1. Most congregations are not familiar with the idea of biblical worship, so it would not be wise to expect a quick acceptance. It could be weeks, months, or even years before the people buy into it.

2. Carefully prepared lessons with ample Scripture should accompany the study.

3. Forced worship is not the pastor's goal or responsibility and would only hurt the church and our Lord.

4. Before you introduce the concept, help your leadership to understand, to be supportive, and to be ready to participate themselves.

5. When you come to the time in the worship service set aside for worship, address the people, explaining that kneeling is the normal biblical form. Explain that if any are not ready to kneel in worship, they may simply join the rest by sitting reverently with heads bowed.

6. Acknowledge that there may be some who cannot physically bow and that God understands their limitations.

7. I would think almost every church has had a prayer service in which the people were asked to kneel. On this worship occasion, remind them of it and invite them to kneel as they have done before to pray, but this time to worship.

8. Assure every member that God wants this to be a very special time with each of His children.

Chapter Fifteen

A Sample Sunday Morning Worship Service

I have always designated Sunday morning for the worship service. To my knowledge, there is no text that specifically mentions it must be on Sunday morning; but whatever service we choose, we should have reasons for our selection.

I offer the following reasons for my position. First, the Scriptures emphasize Sunday morning as the time the early church came together. Second, over the years, I have observed church signs about service times. Without exception, in my recollection, worship services have all been advertised on Sunday morning. Third, when people called our church about Sunday services they would usually ask what time the worship service started. I have also noted that attendance is usually greater on Sunday morning than at any other service. The service that we designate for worship cannot but equate with how important worship is to us. Fourth, I believe the worship act serves as a great witness. Witnessing is something done by the saved in order to reach the lost. In every church, there are probably those who have never had the courage to talk to someone about the Lord. Many of these are good people and are not pleased with themselves about that failure. Every great witness whom I have known still wishes he had witnessed more. Having a time of corporate worship during the service that receives the most visitors is a great opportunity to witness. There may be no greater way for a congregation to convey or to illustrate who and what God is than to worship. A sanctuary full of people on their knees before God is unusual and unmistakable. "Worship is nothing more nor less than love on its knees before the beloved; just as mission is love on its feet to serve the beloved."[1]

The Sunday morning worship service can start like almost any other Sunday morning service. The pastor or music director should open the service by welcoming everyone and inviting them to stand and join in the singing. The title and page number could be given at that time. The first song or two should be uplifting and easy to sing. The goal is to get everyone involved and to capture their minds so their thoughts are on the things of God. Scriptures inserted between songs can add to the service. The third song or at least the fourth should be more directional, leading toward worship. The atmosphere of the time for worship should be of such character that it will be easy for men to think about God and difficult for them to forget Him. For instance, "Holy, Holy, Holy" would be quite appropriate, or "O Worship the King"; "My Jesus, I Love Thee"; "Be Thou My Vision"; "Immortal, Invisible, God Only Wise"; and there are many more choices.

After a verse or two, while the instruments continue to play softly, the music director can address the people concerning worship. He might say something similar to this: "The Sunday morning service is our worship service. As we worship God in song, prayer and praise, let us not forget the most biblical posture for worship, which is to bow. We invite you to come to the altars, bow where you are, or sit reverently in your pew while the instruments play softly. If you are not physically able to bow, God understands. This is a time, not primarily for praying, which is asking, or for praise, which is thanking God, but a time for adoration. The pastor will then close our worship with a prayer, and we will sing the final verse."

When it is time for the offering, it, too, can be incorporated into the worship service. Worship is primarily a verb and is not asking or thanking, but giving. God's people will always find more joy in giving when they view their gifts of finances as going to God rather than to the utility company. Obviously, those expenses must be covered, and the people know it, but there is no harm in reminding them that the tithe and the offering are the Lord's. To illustrate it, the offering could be taken, starting in the back and working to the front. The ushers can then place the plates on the altar and offer a prayer. Placing the gifts of the people before the Lord can warmly seal that part of the service.

When the pastor approaches the pulpit for the preaching time, he can easily keep the people's focus by first proclaiming, "God has chosen preaching for instruction and for reaching the lost. We will honor Him this morning as He has instructed us. Please stand and turn in your Bibles to (chosen text)."

At the close of the message, the invitation time is well suited for another word about worship. "It has been a great morning. We have given honor to our incomparable God in prayer, in song, in worship, and in offerings. Come now and give Him your life, if you have not done so. Above all things you can give, it is **you** He desires most. He loves you and gave His life for you. Everything we have done this morning says come. In the last chapter of the Bible, the Spirit and the Bride say come. Our church family invites you now—come!"

At the close of the invitation and after the altar work is completed, the service comes to an end. I cannot too ardently plead with you to **not** close with announcements. These good people have given of their time, their talent and their resources. Tomorrow, they must once again go out into a sin-cursed world and try to represent Christ. What is it that they need most—a reminder for the ball game that week, or a reminder of a baby shower? No! They need God!

Oh, Pastor, as they stand, looking at you with anxious eyes, give them not the things of the world. With the compassion of the Chief Shepherd Himself, look them in the eye and send them on their way with Acts 20:32, which says: "And now, brethren, I commend you to God, and to the word of his grace, which is able to build you up, and to give you an inheritance among all them which are sanctified." Or maybe Numbers 6:24–26, which says: "The LORD bless thee, and keep thee: The LORD make his face shine upon thee, and be gracious unto thee: The LORD lift up his countenance upon thee, and give thee peace." There are many appropriate scriptures to send them away with God's blessing, as opposed to something secular. If a verse of scripture or a song does not fit, then simply offer a personal word from their under-shepherd: "Go now, and God be with you!"

Appendix A

For sake of illustration, let's compare a church service to a stage play. There are several similarities, beginning with how the building is designed and continuing with those in attendance. First, let's consider what I will refer to as a regular preaching service. The pastor is on the platform, with the congregation seated before him. He is, in the comparison, the actor; the congregation is the audience. In addition, every sincere Bible preacher has implored the Holy Spirit to help him. Our Heavenly Father says He will honor such requests (Luke 11:13). God would fill the part of a production director and will be present, yet out of sight, like a director.

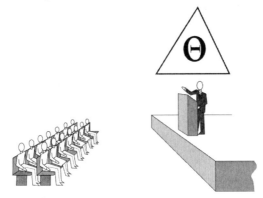

Note: The symbol being used for God is the Greek letter, Theta, the first Greek letter in the word *Theos*, for God. It is incased in a triangle to represent the Trinity.

When we move from a preaching service to a worship service, the players exchange parts. God is the *only* audience for the worship service, so He alone is situated in the main auditorium. The people in the congregation become the actors. The pastor now becomes the director, teaching, encouraging, and illustrating how to worship.

Obviously, the congregation cannot move to the platform, but the sketch is given as such to show that corporate worship is the individual Christian's opportunity to express, in biblical terms, who and what God means to him.

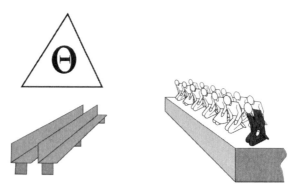

Worship is *the voluntary humbling of one person, physically and spiritually, in order to exalt another.*

Appendix B

Verses on Prayer

Genesis 20:17 So Abraham prayed unto God: and God healed Abimelech, and his wife, and his maidservants; and they bare children.

Genesis 24:12 And he said, O LORD God of my master Abraham, I pray thee, send me good speed this day, and shew kindness unto my master Abraham.

Numbers 11:2 And the people cried unto Moses; and when Moses prayed unto the LORD, the fire was quenched.

Numbers 21:7 Therefore the people came to Moses, and said, We have sinned, for we have spoken against the LORD, and against thee; pray unto the LORD, that he take away the serpents from us. And Moses prayed for the people.

Judges 16:28 And Samson called unto the LORD, and said, O LORD GOD, remember me, I pray thee, and strengthen me, I pray thee, only this once, O God, that I may be at once avenged of the Philistines for my two eyes.

Judges 18:5 And they said unto him, Ask counsel, we pray thee, of God, that we may know whether our way which we go shall be prosperous.

I Samuel 1:12 And it came to pass, as she continued praying before the LORD, that Eli marked her mouth.

I Samuel 1:27 For this child I prayed; and the LORD hath given me my petition which I asked of him:

II Samuel 15:31 And one told David, saying, Ahithophel is among the conspirators with Absalom. And David said, O Lord, I pray thee, turn the counsel of Ahithophel into foolishness.

I Kings 8:26 And now, O God of Israel, let thy word, I pray thee, be verified, which thou spakest unto thy servant David my father.

I Kings 8:54 And it was so, that when Solomon had made an end of praying all this prayer and supplication unto the Lord, he arose from before the altar of the Lord, from kneeling on his knees with his hands spread up to heaven.

I Kings 9:3 And the Lord said unto him, I have heard thy prayer and thy supplication, that thou hast made before me: I have hallowed this house, which thou hast built, to put my name there for ever; and mine eyes and mine heart shall be there perpetually.

I Kings 13:6 And the king answered and said unto the man of God, Intreat now the face of the Lord thy God, and pray for me, that my hand may be restored me again. And the man of God besought the Lord, and the king's hand was restored him again, and became as it was before.

I Kings 17:21 And he stretched himself upon the child three times, and cried unto the Lord, and said, O Lord my God, I pray thee, let this child's soul come into him again.

II Kings 6:17, 18 And Elisha prayed, and said, Lord, I pray thee, open his eyes, that he may see. And the Lord opened the eyes of the young man; and he saw: and, behold, the mountain was full of horses and chariots of fire round about Elisha. And when they came down to him, Elisha prayed unto the Lord, and said, Smite this people, I pray thee, with blindness. And he smote them with blindness according to the word of Elisha.

II Kings 20:5 Turn again, and tell Hezekiah the captain of my people, Thus saith the Lord, the God of David thy father, I have heard thy prayer, I have seen thy tears: behold, I will heal thee: on the third day thou shalt go up unto the house of the Lord.

II Chronicles 6:19 Have respect therefore to the prayer of thy servant, and to his supplication, O Lord my God, to hearken unto the cry and the prayer which thy servant prayeth before thee:

II Chronicles 6:29 Then what prayer or what supplication soever shall be made of any man, or of all thy people Israel, when every one shall know his own sore and his own grief, and shall spread forth his hands in this house:

II Chronicles 6:35 Then hear thou from the heavens their prayer and their supplication, and maintain their cause.

II Chronicles 6:39 Then hear thou from the heavens, even from thy dwelling place, their prayer and their supplications, and maintain their cause, and forgive thy people which have sinned against thee.

II Chronicles 7:1 Now when Solomon had made an end of praying, the fire came down from heaven, and consumed the burnt-offering and the sacrifices; and the glory of the LORD filled the house.

II Chronicles 7:12 And the LORD appeared to Solomon by night, and said unto him, I have heard thy prayer, and have chosen this place to myself for an house of sacrifice.

II Chronicles 7:14, 15 If my people, which are called by my name, shall humble themselves, and pray, and seek my face, and turn from their wicked ways; then will I hear from heaven, and will forgive their sin, and will heal their land. Now mine eyes shall be open, and mine ears attent unto the prayer that is made in this place.

Nehemiah 1:6 Let thine ear now be attentive, and thine eyes open, that thou mayest hear the prayer of thy servant, which I pray before thee now, day and night, for the children of Israel thy servants, and confess the sins of the children of Israel, which we have sinned against thee: both I and my father's house have sinned.

Nehemiah 1:11 O LORD, I beseech thee, let now thine ear be attentive to the prayer of thy servant, and to the prayer of thy servants, who desire to fear thy name: and prosper, I pray thee, thy servant this day, and grant him mercy in the sight of this man. For I was the king's cupbearer.

Psalm 4:1 Hear me when I call, O God of my righteousness: thou hast enlarged me when I was in distress; have mercy upon me, and hear my prayer.

Psalm 5:3 My voice shalt thou hear in the morning, O LORD; in the morning will I direct my prayer unto thee, and will look up.

Psalm 54:2 Hear my prayer, O God; give ear to the words of my mouth.

Psalm 55:1 Give ear to my prayer, O God; and hide not thyself from my supplication.

Psalm 61:1 Hear my cry, O God; attend unto my prayer.

Psalm 64:1 Hear my voice, O God, in my prayer: preserve my life from fear of the enemy.

Psalm 69:13 But as for me, my prayer is unto thee, O LORD, in an acceptable time: O God, in the multitude of thy mercy hear me, in the truth of thy salvation.

Psalm 86:6 Give ear, O LORD, unto my prayer; and attend to the voice of my supplications.

Psalm 142:1 I cried unto the LORD with my voice; with my voice unto the LORD did I make my supplication.

Psalm 143:1 Hear my prayer, O LORD, give ear to my supplications: in thy faithfulness answer me, and in thy righteousness.

Proverbs 15:29 The LORD is far from the wicked: but he heareth the prayer of the righteous.

Isaiah 38:5 Go, and say to Hezekiah, Thus saith the LORD, the God of David thy father, I have heard thy prayer, I have seen thy tears: behold, I will add unto thy days fifteen years.

Daniel 9:17 Now therefore, O our God, hear the prayer of thy servant, and his supplications, and cause thy face to shine upon thy sanctuary that is desolate, for the Lord's sake.

Daniel 9:21 Yea, whiles I was speaking in prayer, even the man Gabriel, whom I had seen in the vision at the beginning, being caused to fly swiftly, touched me about the time of the evening oblation.

Jonah 2:7 When my soul fainted within me I remembered the LORD: and my prayer came in unto thee, into thine holy temple.

Matthew 21:22 And all things, whatsoever ye shall ask in prayer, believing, ye shall receive.

Mark 9:29 And he said unto them, This kind can come forth by nothing, but by prayer and fasting.

Luke 1:13, 14 But the angel said unto him, Fear not, Zacharias: for thy prayer is heard; and thy wife Elisabeth shall bear thee a son, and thou shalt call his name John. And thou shalt have joy and gladness; and many shall rejoice at his birth.

Acts 12:5 Peter therefore was kept in prison: but prayer was made without ceasing of the church unto God for him.

Acts 16:13 And on the sabbath we went out of the city by a river side, where prayer was wont to be made; and we sat down, and spake unto the women which resorted thither.

Romans 10:1 Brethren, my heart's desire and prayer to God for Israel is, that they might be saved.

II Corinthians 1:11 Ye also helping together by prayer for us, that for the gift bestowed upon us by the means of many persons thanks may be given by many on our behalf.

Philippians 1:4 Always in every prayer of mine for you all making request with joy,

Philippians 4:6 Be careful for nothing; but in every thing by prayer and supplication with thanksgiving let your requests be made known unto God.

Colossians 4:12 Epaphras, who is one of you, a servant of Christ, saluteth you, always labouring fervently for you in prayers, that ye may stand perfect and complete in all the will of God.

Philemon 1:22 But withal prepare me also a lodging: for I trust that through your prayers I shall be given unto you.

James 5:15, 16 And the prayer of faith shall save the sick, and the Lord shall raise him up; and if he have committed sins, they shall be forgiven him. Confess your faults one to another, and pray one for another, that ye may be healed. The effectual fervent prayer of a righteous man availeth much.

I Peter 3:7 Likewise, ye husbands, dwell with them according to knowledge, giving honour unto the wife, as unto the weaker vessel, and as being heirs together of the grace of life; that your prayers be not hindered.

I Peter 3:12 For the eyes of the Lord are over the righteous, and his ears are open unto their prayers: but the face of the LORD is against them that do evil.

Verses on Praise

Judges 5:2 Praise ye the LORD for the avenging of Israel, when the people willingly offered themselves.

I Chronicles 16:35 And say ye, Save us, O God of our salvation, and gather us together, and deliver us from the heathen, that we may give thanks to thy holy name, and glory in thy praise.

I Chronicles 23:30 And to stand every morning to thank and praise the LORD, and likewise at even;

I Chronicles 25:3 Of Jeduthun: the sons of Jeduthun; Gedaliah, and Zeri, and Jeshaiah, Hashabiah, and Mattithiah, six, under the hands of their father Jeduthun, who prophesied with a harp, to give thanks and to praise the LORD.

I Chronicles 29:13 Now therefore, our God, we thank thee, and praise thy glorious name.

II Chronicles 7:6 And the priests waited on their offices: the Levites also with instruments of musick of the LORD, which David the king had made to praise the LORD, because his mercy endureth for ever, when David praised by their ministry; and the priests sounded trumpets before them, and all Israel stood.

II Chronicles 20:21 And when he had consulted with the people, he appointed singers unto the LORD, and that should praise the beauty of holiness, as they went out before the army, and to say, Praise the LORD; for his mercy endureth for ever.

II Chronicles 29:30 Moreover Hezekiah the king and the princes commanded the Levites to sing praise unto the LORD with the words of David, and of Asaph the seer. And they sang praises with gladness, and they bowed their heads and worshipped.

Nehemiah 12:24 And the chief of the Levites: Hashabiah, Sherebiah, and Jeshua the son of Kadmiel, with their brethren over against them, to praise and to give thanks, according to the commandment of David the man of God, ward over against ward.

Nehemiah 12:46 For in the days of David and Asaph of old there were chief of the singers, and songs of praise and thanksgiving unto God.

Psalm 9:14 That I may shew forth all thy praise in the gates of the daughter of Zion: I will rejoice in thy salvation.

Psalm 28:7 The LORD is my strength and my shield; my heart trusted in him, and I am helped: therefore my heart greatly rejoiceth; and with my song will I praise him.

Psalm 30:12 To the end that my glory may sing praise to thee, and not be silent. O LORD my God, I will give thanks unto thee for ever.

Psalm 42:11 Why art thou cast down, O my soul? and why art thou disquieted within me? hope thou in God: for I shall yet praise him, who is the health of my countenance, and my God.

Psalm 43:5 Why art thou cast down, O my soul? and why art thou disquieted within me? hope in God: for I shall yet praise him, who is the health of my countenance, and my God.

Psalm 52:9 I will praise thee for ever, because thou hast done it: and I will wait on thy name; for it is good before thy saints.

Psalm 63:5 My soul shall be satisfied as with marrow and fatness; and my mouth shall praise thee with joyful lips:

Psalm 69:30 I will praise the name of God with a song, and will magnify him with thanksgiving.

Psalm 71:6 By thee have I been holden up from the womb: thou art he that took me out of my mother's bowels: my praise shall be continually of thee.

Psalm 89:5 And the heavens shall praise thy wonders, O LORD: thy faithfulness also in the congregation of the saints.

Psalm 100:4 Enter into his gates with thanksgiving, and into his courts with praise: be thankful unto him, and bless his name.

Psalm 106:1 Praise ye the LORD. O give thanks unto the LORD; for he is good: for his mercy endureth for ever.

Psalm 106:47 Save us, O Lord our God, and gather us from among the heathen, to give thanks unto thy holy name, and to triumph in thy praise.

Psalm 107:8 Oh that men would praise the Lord for his goodness, and for his wonderful works to the children of men!

Psalm 113:9 He maketh the barren woman to keep house, and to be a joyful mother of children. Praise ye the Lord.

Psalm 117:2 For his merciful kindness is great toward us: and the truth of the Lord endureth for ever. Praise ye the Lord.

Psalm 118:19 Open to me the gates of righteousness: I will go into them, and I will praise the Lord:

Psalm 118:21 I will praise thee: for thou hast heard me, and art become my salvation.

Psalm 119:7 I will praise thee with uprightness of heart, when I shall have learned thy righteous judgments.

Psalm 119:164 Seven times a day do I praise thee because of thy righteous judgments.

Psalm 119:171 My lips shall utter praise, when thou hast taught me thy statutes.

Psalm 119:175 Let my soul live, and it shall praise thee; and let thy judgments help me.

Psalm 138:2 I will worship toward thy holy temple, and praise thy name for thy lovingkindness and for thy truth: for thou hast magnified thy word above all thy name.

Psalm 138:4 All the kings of the earth shall praise thee, O Lord, when they hear the words of thy mouth.

Psalm 139:14 I will praise thee; for I am fearfully and wonderfully made: marvellous are thy works; and that my soul knoweth right well.

Psalm 142:7 Bring my soul out of prison, that I may praise thy name: the righteous shall compass me about; for thou shalt deal bountifully with me.

Psalm 145:4 One generation shall praise thy works to another, and shall declare thy mighty acts.

Psalm 145:10 All thy works shall praise thee, O Lord; and thy saints shall bless thee.

Psalm 147:7 Sing unto the Lord with thanksgiving; sing praise upon the harp unto our God:

Psalm 147:20 He hath not dealt so with any nation: and as for his judgments, they have not known them. Praise ye the LORD.

Psalm 149:9 To execute upon them the judgment written: this honour have all his saints. Praise ye the LORD.

Psalm 150:2 Praise him for his mighty acts: praise him according to his excellent greatness.

Isaiah 12:1 And in that day thou shalt say, O LORD, I will praise thee: though thou wast angry with me, thine anger is turned away, and thou comfortedst me.

Isaiah 12: 4 And in that day shall ye say, Praise the LORD, call upon his name, declare his doings among the people, make mention that his name is exalted.

Isaiah 25:1 O LORD, thou art my God; I will exalt thee, I will praise thy name; for thou hast done wonderful things; thy counsels of old are faithfulness and truth.

Isaiah 62:9 But they that have gathered it shall eat it, and praise the LORD; and they that have brought it together shall drink it in the courts of my holiness.

Jeremiah 17:14 Heal me, O LORD, and I shall be healed; save me, and I shall be saved: for thou art my praise.

Jeremiah 20:13 Sing unto the LORD, praise ye the LORD: for he hath delivered the soul of the poor from the hand of evildoers.

Jeremiah 33:11 The voice of joy, and the voice of gladness, the voice of the bridegroom, and the voice of the bride, the voice of them that shall say, Praise the LORD of hosts: for the LORD is good; for his mercy endureth for ever: and of them that shall bring the sacrifice of praise into the house of the LORD. For I will cause to return the captivity of the land, as at the first, saith the LORD.

Daniel 2:23 I thank thee, and praise thee, O thou God of my fathers, who hast given me wisdom and might, and hast made known unto me now what we desired of thee: for thou hast now made known unto us the king's matter.

Daniel 4:37 Now I Nebuchadnezzar praise and extol and honour the King of heaven, all whose works are truth, and his ways judgment: and those that walk in pride he is able to abase.

Joel 2:26 And ye shall eat in plenty, and be satisfied, and praise the name of the LORD your God, that hath dealt wondrously with you: and my people shall never be ashamed.

Luke 18:43 And immediately he received his sight, and followed him, glorifying God: and all the people, when they saw it, gave praise unto God.

Luke 19:37 And when he was come nigh, even now at the descent of the mount of Olives, the whole multitude of the disciples began to rejoice and praise God with a loud voice for all the mighty works that they had seen;

Verses on Worship

Genesis 22:5 And Abraham said unto his young men, Abide ye here with the ass; and I and the lad will go yonder and worship, and come again to you.

Genesis 24:26, 28, 52 And the man bowed down his head, and worshipped the LORD. ... And the damsel ran, and told them of her mother's house these things. ... And it came to pass, that, when Abraham's servant heard their words, he worshipped the LORD, bowing himself to the earth.

Exodus 4:31 And the people believed: and when they heard that the LORD had visited the children of Israel, and that he had looked upon their affliction, then they bowed their heads and worshipped.

Exodus 24:1 And he said unto Moses, Come up unto the LORD, thou, and Aaron, Nadab, and Abihu, and seventy of the elders of Israel; and worship ye afar off.

Exodus 33:10 And all the people saw the cloudy pillar stand at the tabernacle door: and all the people rose up and worshipped, every man in his tent door.

Exodus 34:8 And Moses made haste, and bowed his head toward the earth, and worshipped.

Deuteronomy 11:16 Take heed to yourselves, that your heart be not deceived, and ye turn aside, and serve other gods, and worship them;

I Samuel 1:3, 19 And this man went up out of his city yearly to worship and to sacrifice unto the LORD of hosts in Shiloh. And the two sons of Eli, Hophni and Phinehas, the priests of the LORD, were there. ... And they rose up in the morning early, and worshipped before the LORD, and returned, and came to their house to Ramah: and Elkanah knew Hannah his wife; and the LORD remembered her.

I Samuel 1:28 Therefore also I have lent him to the LORD; as long as he liveth he shall be lent to the LORD. And he worshipped the LORD there.

II Samuel 12:20 Then David arose from the earth, and washed, and anointed himself, and changed his apparel, and came into the house of the LORD, and worshipped: then he came to his own house; and when he required, they set bread before him, and he did eat.

II Samuel 15:32 And it came to pass, that when David was come to the top of the mount, where he worshipped God, behold, Hushai the Archite came to meet him with his coat rent, and earth upon his head:

II Kings 17:36 But the Lord, who brought you up out of the land of Egypt with great power and a stretched out arm, him shall ye fear, and him shall ye worship, and to him shall ye do sacrifice.

I Chronicles 16:29 Give unto the Lord the glory due unto his name: bring an offering, and come before him: worship the Lord in the beauty of holiness.

I Chronicles 29:20 And David said to all the congregation, Now bless the Lord your God. And all the congregation blessed the Lord God of their fathers, and bowed down their heads, and worshipped the Lord, and the king.

II Chronicles 7:3 And when all the children of Israel saw how the fire came down, and the glory of the Lord upon the house, they bowed themselves with their faces to the ground upon the pavement, and worshipped, and praised the Lord, saying, For he is good; for his mercy endureth for ever.

II Chronicles 29:28–30 And all the congregation worshipped, and the singers sang, and the trumpeters sounded: and all this continued until the burnt offering was finished. And when they had made an end of offering, the king and all that were present with him bowed themselves, and worshipped. Moreover Hezekiah the king and the princes commanded the Levites to sing praise unto the Lord with the words of David, and of Asaph the seer. And they sang praises with gladness, and they bowed their heads and worshipped.

Nehemiah 8:6 And Ezra blessed the Lord, the great God. And all the people answered, Amen, Amen, with lifting up their hands: and they bowed their heads, and worshipped the Lord with their faces to the ground.

Nehemiah 9:3 And they stood up in their place, and read in the book of the law of the Lord their God one fourth part of the day; and another fourth part they confessed, and worshipped the Lord their God.

Job 1:20 Then Job arose, and rent his mantle, and shaved his head, and fell down upon the ground, and worshipped.

Psalm 5:7 But as for me, I will come into thy house in the multitude of thy mercy: and in thy fear will I worship toward thy holy temple.

Psalm 22:27 All the ends of the world shall remember and turn unto the Lord: and all the kindreds of the nations shall worship before thee.

Psalm 29:2 Give unto the Lord the glory due unto his name; worship the Lord in the beauty of holiness.

Psalm 45:11 So shall the king greatly desire thy beauty: for he is thy Lord; and worship thou him.

Psalm 95:6 O come, let us worship and bow down: let us kneel before the Lord our maker.

Psalm 96:9 O worship the Lord in the beauty of holiness: fear before him, all the earth.

Psalm 99:5 Exalt ye the Lord our God, and worship at his footstool; for he is holy.

Psalm 99:9 Exalt the Lord our God, and worship at his holy hill; for the Lord our God is holy.

Psalm 132:7 We will go into his tabernacles: we will worship at his footstool.

Isaiah 27:13 And it shall come to pass in that day, that the great trumpet shall be blown, and they shall come which were ready to perish in the land of Assyria, and the outcasts in the land of Egypt, and shall worship the Lord in the holy mount at Jerusalem.

Isaiah 66:23 And it shall come to pass, that from one new moon to another, and from one sabbath to another, shall all flesh come to worship before me, saith the Lord.

Jeremiah 7:2 Stand in the gate of the Lord's house, and proclaim there this word, and say, Hear the word of the Lord, all ye of Judah, that enter in at these gates to worship the Lord.

Jeremiah 26:2 Thus saith the Lord; Stand in the court of the Lord's house, and speak unto all the cities of Judah, which come to worship in the Lord's house, all the words that I command thee to speak unto them; diminish not a word:

Ezekiel 46:3, 9 Likewise the people of the land shall worship at the door of this gate before the Lord in the sabbaths and in the new moons. ... But when the people of the land shall come before the Lord in the solemn feasts, he that entereth in by the way of the north gate to worship shall go out by the way of the south gate; and he that entereth by the way of the south gate shall go forth by the way of the north gate: he shall not return by the way of the gate whereby he came in, but shall go forth over against it.

Daniel 2:46 Then the king Nebuchadnezzar fell upon his face, and worshipped Daniel, and commanded that they should offer an oblation and sweet odours unto him.

Zephaniah 2:11 The Lord will be terrible unto them: for he will famish all the gods of the earth; and men shall worship him, every one from his place, even all the isles of the heathen.

Matthew 2:2, 11 Saying, Where is he that is born King of the Jews? for we have seen his star in the east, and are come to worship him. ... And when they were come into the house, they saw the young child with Mary his mother, and fell down, and worshipped him: and when they had opened their treasures, they presented unto him gifts; gold, and frankincense, and myrrh.

Matthew 4:10 Then saith Jesus unto him, Get thee hence, Satan: for it is written, THOU SHALT WORSHIP THE LORD THY GOD, AND HIM ONLY SHALT THOU SERVE.

Matthew 14:33 Then they that were in the ship came and worshipped him, saying, Of a truth thou art the Son of God.

Matthew 15:9 BUT IN VAIN THEY DO WORSHIP ME, TEACHING FOR DOCTRINES THE COMMANDMENTS OF MEN.

Matthew 15:25 Then came she and worshipped him, saying, Lord, help me.

Matthew 28:9, 17 And as they went to tell his disciples, behold, Jesus met them, saying, All hail. And they came and held him by the feet, and worshipped him. ... And when they saw him, they worshipped him: but some doubted.

Mark 5:6 But when he saw Jesus afar off, he ran and worshipped him,

Luke 24:52 And they worshipped him, and returned to Jerusalem with great joy:

John 4:22–24 Ye worship ye know not what: we know what we worship: for salvation is of the Jews. But the hour cometh, and now is, when the true worshippers shall worship the Father in spirit and in truth: for the Father seeketh such to worship him. God is a Spirit: and they that worship him must worship him in spirit and in truth.

John 9:38 And he said, Lord, I believe. And he worshipped him.

Acts 16:14 And a certain woman named Lydia, a seller of purple, of the city of Thyatira, which worshipped God, heard us: whose heart the LORD opened, that she attended unto the things which were spoken of Paul.

Acts 18:7 And he departed thence, and entered into a certain man's house, named Justus, one that worshipped God, whose house joined hard to the synagogue.

Acts 24:14 But this I confess unto thee, that after the way which they call heresy, so worship I the God of my fathers, believing all things which are written in the law and in the prophets:

I Corinthians 14:25 And thus are the secrets of his heart made manifest; and so falling down on his face he will worship God, and report that God is in you of a truth.

Philippians 3:3 For we are the circumcision, which worship God in the spirit, and rejoice in Christ Jesus, and have no confidence in the flesh.

Hebrews 1:6 And again, when he bringeth in the firstbegotten into the world, he saith, AND LET ALL THE ANGELS OF GOD WORSHIP HIM.

Revelation 4:10, 11 The four and twenty elders fall down before him that sat on the throne, and worship him that liveth for ever and ever, and cast their crowns before the throne, saying, Thou art worthy, O Lord, to receive glory and honour and power: for thou hast created all things, and for thy pleasure they are and were created.

Revelation 5:14 And the four beasts said, Amen. And the four and twenty elders fell down and worshipped him that liveth for ever and ever.

Revelation 7:11 And all the angels stood round about the throne, and about the elders and the four beasts, and fell before the throne on their faces, and worshipped God,

Revelation 11:16 And the four and twenty elders, which sat before God on their seats, fell upon their faces, and worshipped God,

Revelation 14:7 Saying with a loud voice, Fear God, and give glory to him; for the hour of his judgment is come: and worship him that made heaven, and earth, and the sea, and the fountains of waters.

Revelation 15:4 Who shall not fear thee, O Lord, and glorify thy name? for thou only art holy: for all nations shall come and worship before thee; for thy judgments are made manifest.

Revelation 19:4 And the four and twenty elders and the four beasts fell down and worshipped God that sat on the throne, saying, Amen; Alleluia.

Revelation 19:10 And I fell at his feet to worship him. And he said unto me, See thou do it not: I am thy fellowservant, and of thy brethren that have the testimony of Jesus: worship God: for the testimony of Jesus is the spirit of prophecy.

Notes

Chapter One: The Journey to Worship Begins

1. Frank S. Mead, *The Encyclopedia of Religious Quotations* (Grand Rapids: Fleming H. Revell Co., 1965), 479.

Chapter Three: A Definition of Worship

1. J.D. Douglas, *The New Bible Dictionary* (Westmont, Illinois: InterVarsity Press, 1982), 1262.

2. Walter Bauer, F. Wilbur Gingrich, William F. Arndt, Frederick W. Danker, *A Greek-English Lexicon of the New Testament and Other Early Christian Literature* (Chicago: University of Chicago Press, 2001), 716.

3. James Strong, *The Exhaustive Concordance of the Bible* (Cincinnati: Jennings & Graham, 1890), 1190.

4. Ronald B. Allen and Dr. Gordon Borror, *Worship: Rediscovering the Missing Jewel* (Eugene, Oregon: Wipf & Stock Publishers, 1982), 16.

5. Everitt F. Harrison, *Baker's Dictionary of Theology* (Grand Rapids: Baker Book House, 1960), 560.

Chapter Four: The Attitude of Worship

1. Piercarlo Valdesolo and Jesse Graham, "Awe, Uncertainty, and Agency Detection" (*Psychological Science*, November 25, 2013).

2. Edythe Draper, ed., *Draper's Book of Quotations for the Christian World* (Wheaton: Tyndale House Publishers, 1992), 657.

3. H.H. Rowley, *Worship in Ancient Israel: Its Forms and Meanings* (Eugene, Oregon: Wipf & Stock Publishers, 1967), 257.

4. Ibid., 270.

5. Warren Wiersbe, *The Bible Exposition Commentary, New Testament, Vol. 1* (Colorado Springs: Chariot Victor Publishing, 1992), 180.

Chapter Five: Elements and Uniqueness of Worship

1. *McGraw-Hill Dictionary of American Idioms and Phrasal Verbs* (New York City: The McGraw-Hill Companies, Inc., 2002).

2. Alfred P. Gibbs, *Worship: The Christian's Highest Occupation* (Kansas City: Walterick Publishers, 1950), 26.

3. R. Laird Harris and Gleason L. Archer, Jr., *Theological Wordbook of the Old Testament* (Chicago: Moody Publishers, 1980), 217, 364.

4. Merrill C. Tenney, editor, *Zondervan Pictorial Encyclopedia of the Bible, Vol. 4* (Grand Rapids: Zondervan Publishing, 1980), 834.

5. Charles H. Spurgeon, *The Metropolitan Tabernacle Pulpit: Vol.8* (London: Passmore and Alabaster, 1862), 107.

6. M.A. Leiper, ed., *Language Works in Elementary Schools* (Boston: The Athenaeym Press, 1916), 267.

7. Albert M. Wells, Jr., *Inspiring Quotations* (Nashville: Thomas Nelson Publishers, 1988), 201.

8. Ibid., 202.

9. Edward M. Deems, *Holy-Days and Holidays* (New York: Funk & Wagnalls Company, 1902), 369.

10. Immanuel Kant, *Critique of Practical Reason*, quoted in John Bartlett's *Bartlett's Familiar Quotations* (Boston: Little, Brown & Company, 1892), 366.

Chapter Seven: The Object of Worship

1. Warren Wiersbe, *The Best of A.W. Tozer* (Harrisburg, Pennsylvania: Christian Publications, Inc., 1973), 14.

2. "Comin' In on a Wing and a Prayer" is a World War II song with lyrics by Harold Adamson and music by Jimmy McHugh, published in 1943 by Robbins Music Corp. The song was famously recorded by The Song Spinners for Decca Records, reaching No. 1 on the Billboard pop chart on July 2, 1943. "Comin' In on a Wing and a Prayer" was the only song with a war connection to appear in the top twenty best-selling songs of 1943 in the United States, bearing in mind that 1943 was affected by the first Petrillo recording ban.

3. A. W. Tozer, *Tozer on Worship and Entertainment* (Chicago: Moody Publishers, 2006 reprint), 1.

4. G. Campbell Morgan, *The Crisis of the Christ* (London: Fleming H. Revell Company, 1903), 42.

5. Benjamin Disraeli, *The Novels of Benjamin Disraeli* (G. Routledge and Sons, 1888), 109.

6. Tryon Edwards, D.D., *The New Dictionary of Thoughts* (New York: Standard Book, 1957), 744.

Chapter Eight: The Law of First Mention

1. C.S. Lewis, *The Lion, the Witch, and the Wardrobe* (Greenwich, Connecticut: Touchstone Publishers, 1996), 93.

Chapter Ten: Worship and Grace

1. Alexander MacLaren, *MacLaren's Commentary—Expositions of Holy Scriptures, Vol. 14* (Grand Rapids: Baker Book House, 1977), 217.

2. Paul David Tripp, *Dangerous Calling* (Wheaton: Crossway Books, 2012), 114.

Chapter Eleven: The Witness of Worship

1. Philip Hughes, *The True Image* (Grand Rapids: Wm. B. Eerdmans Publishing Company, 1989), 56.

Chapter Twelve: The Conflict of Culture and Worship

1. Frederick Dale Bruner, *The Christbook* (Waco, Texas: World Book Publishers, 1987), 112.

2. A.W. Tozer, *Success and the Christian: The Cost of Spiritual Maturity* (Camp Hill, Pennsylvania: Wing Spread Publishers, 2006), 5.

Chapter Thirteen: Worship and Revival

1. Alexander MacLaren, *MacLaren's Commentary—Expositions of Holy Scriptures, Vol. 14* (Grand Rapids: Baker Book House, 1977), 217.

2. Ralph Waldo Emerson, T*he Complete Works of Ralph Waldo Emerson: Comprising His Essays, Lectures, Poems, and Orations, Vol. 2* (London: Bell & Daldy, 1866), 201.

Chapter Fourteen: A Biblical Format for Worship Services

1. Alexander Whyte, *Bible Characters from the Old Testament and the New Testament, Vol. 1, Series 3* (Grand Rapids: Zondervan Publishing House, 1967), 433.

Chapter Fifteen: A Sample Sunday Morning Worship Service

1. N.T. Wright, *For All God's Worth* (Grand Rapids: Wm. B. Eerdmans Publishing Company, 1997), 8.